MW00962620

RadarScan
Issues
Management

By Mark E. Affleck

Issue Action Publications 1998

Issue Action Publications, Inc.
207 Loudoun Street, SE
Leesburg, Virginia 20175
United States of America
Telephone (703) 777-8450

Library of Congress Catalog Card Number: 97-077222
ISBN 0-913869-06-6
First Printing: March 1998

TABLE OF CONTENTS

Acknowledgements

The author wishes to thank:

George Farrelly,
   for his belief and trust in me;

The California Avocado Industry,
   for its incredible support;

Gregg Payne,
   for his insights and direction; and

Teresa Yancey Crane,
   *for her vision and tireless work to
   put issues management "on the map."*

Preface

I became an issues manager the day I became president of the California Avocado Commission in 1988 and I've been at it ever since. What I've learned managing dozens of issues over 10 years is how important it is to get involved early and **act**, even when it doesn't feel right...to anticipate issues, paint scenarios and project trajectories. We all have the ability to do this. We're experts in our own worlds and great at the day-to-day nuts and bolts of running the business, but often we don't think strategically about the future and its forces, trends and emerging issues.

Three years ago, the California avocado industry, faced with a 239 percent increase in water rates, was struggling with the prospect of extinction.

The Southern California Metropolitan Water District (MWD), the world's largest water wholesaler, had raised rates to cover income losses from a lingering, statewide drought. Capital was also needed to finance critical system maintenance and infrastructure expansion. The decision-making process had excluded agriculture, however, one of the agency's most reliable clients. We were largely impotent— and at great risk—in a game in which escalating costs were taken as a given. In fact, if the MWD board had voted early in the process on a rate relief package for agriculture, we would have lost 50 - 1.

But by identifying the issue early and plotting its trajectory, we believed there was an opportunity to launch an education campaign that would bring us effectively back onto the field of play.

Despite opposition from our board of directors, we kept the issue alive, arguing that it was irresponsible not to engage in a dialog to examine our options. The clay was still malleable, and the earlier you get started on an issue, the better odds you have of prevailing.

Our plan was to rally around three arguments:
1) Agriculture contributed mightily to the capitalization of the original system infrastructure, and shouldn't be responsible for demands generated by the urban users who followed.
2) The reduction or demise of agriculture would have significant, negative environmental and economic impacts.

3) Agriculture was being crushed by a factor we labeled "rateshock," the unfair nature of hyper rate increases imposed on an industry, without providing sufficient warning time to adjust.

Our decision to aggressively protect our interests produced an extensive education campaign, involving development of relationships with key MWD board members, and compelling communication pieces. The support of growers was enlisted to convey the message with the passion known only by a person about to lose a lifetime's work and a heritage. And it worked! Three years later, in an historic pact between a utility and customer group, the MWD board voted 50-1 to adopt a three-year agricultural rebate program for avocado growers and the rest of Southern California agriculture. Savings to our industry totaled $59 million over the three years.

Finished project? Never. The hard work continues as we seek a long-term deal to succeed the current interim program. We actually started work on the long-term deal the day following announcement of the interim victory. Working with MWD, helping each other spot problems and issues early, we crafted mutually acceptable responses, resulting in a five-year, $100 million deal to take effect upon expiration of the three-year pact. By starting early with wet clay, we not only secured the long-term deal before completion of the interim pact, but also were part of a process that may well have saved the industry. That's RadarScan Issues Management.

Facing life and death issues seems to be a common occurrence for the California avocado industry. One day it's a water threat, the next, the specter of pest-infested imports flooding the market. That was the case in 1996 when the United States Department of Agriculture (USDA) announced plans to relax a scientifically based quarantine that, since 1914, had barred fresh Mexican avocados from the U.S. As with water, the issue threatened to eradicate the entire $1 billion industry investment.

Fortunately, our RadarScan Issue Management process revealed the problem early, allowing an anticipatory, aggressive, multi-faceted counter attack to be launched. What were the warning signals? As early as 1988, it became clear from media reports and other sources that the U.S. government would eventually abandon its scientifically based exclusion policy of keeping dangerous pests out no matter what, in favor a softer, politically inspired approach that would accept greater risk of pest infestation in order to expand trade and make the North American Free Trade Agreement "work."

We responded by working with top U.S. scientists at major universities to develop the most complete scientific case possible. We developed Mexican sources, scouts in that country looking for compliance and enforcement flaws in Mexico's pest control regulatory structure.

On the legislative track, we worked hard to educate members of Congress on the issue and the scientific support for keeping the quarantine in place. So when the USDA moved to relax the quarantine in early 1996, we were positioned to effectively fight back. Against all odds, the USDA took the matter off the docket in late 1996. Industry savings are incalculable. We avoided a potential death blow from pest infestation, and experts have estimated that price degradation following admission of Mexican fruit could have been as much as $40 million.

Case closed? Again, not by a long shot. The government eventually allowed Mexican imports into the Northeastern U.S. under limited conditions. Our strategy remains the same...anticipate the next move, plot its trajectory and paint scenarios to always be "early." Plans for marketing alliances and partnerships are underway as we adapt to this issue.

Issues and forces. Identify issues and forces and transform the business while there is a chance to do it. It works. I try to look several moves into the future, anticipating lags, reactions, feedback, political shifts and more. My goal is to be in the game, experimenting, making decisions, driving the tractor, moving dirt around to see what's underneath. The key? *Doing* something about forces and issues *early*, not just acknowledging their existence. It's easy to talk about them, but it's much more difficult to make a move, especially early.

Taken to an extreme, actions of Microsoft, the giant software king, defines what it means to move early. Microsoft doesn't wait for anything. It creates the future itself. Think about that for a minute. Think about Microsoft's massive world-wide roll-out and positioning of the Windows 95 operating system. Microsoft boldly forges the road, experimenting and seeking along the way. One of the results is that Microsoft has none of its engineers engaged in changing light bulbs, because the company has redefined what it means to be left in the dark.

This book is about being "on time." Its purpose is to establish the importance of an early orientation to issues management and, perhaps more importantly, early action. The book contains three sections, outlined below:

FIRST: "Playing in the Future Now," a look at why it's important to look at issues management from the early perspective and how to organize your resources to make it happen.

SECOND: The six-part "RadarScan" Issues Management Model which formalizes the process of looking for the issues that will impact the organization and developing techniques to manage them. The Model consists of these six elements:
- **Soul** - *What does the organization stand for now? What does it want to be in the future?*
- **Scan** - *What will sink the ship? What are the Strategic Impact Issues?*
- **Analyze** - *Where is the issue on the life cycle? Who are the targets? What are the results of the Probability/Impact/Risk Assessment?*
- **Strategy** - *What are the organization's goals? What are the Response Options? What resources are available?*
- **Action** - *What should the organization's response be? How do the stakeholders feel about the issue? How should the communication program be constructed?*
- **Review** - *What evaluation tools should we use? How did the issues management program perform at mid-point? At program conclusion?*

THIRD: "Begin to Begin...Take Action," covers the importance of doing something that will transform the issue for your organization. The focus here is on putting in play strategies and tactics that will move the issue toward a resolution which mutually benefits all stakeholders involved.

The book is built on the following Foundation Tenets:
- There is "no such thing as on time." There is only early and late.
- Traditional, linear structure doesn't work well in an amorphous, virtual environment.
- It may be true, as the hippie said, that everybody has to be somewhere....but soul's the secret to getting where you want to be.
- There are better options than probable death and certain death.
- People may be created equal, but information is NOT.
- Everything is composed of relationships...and they are always more convoluted than you thought they were.

- It's a lot more like skeet shooting than firing at still targets; everything has a distressing tendency to keep moving.
- You've succeeded if, in the end, they believe they won.
- If you don't know where you are and if you don't know where you've been, arriving where you want to be becomes an improbable accident of sheer, dumb luck.
- Take action and go!

We're entering the most challenging and exciting time in modern day business history and the need for issues management is growing exponentially. The new frontier dawning is a "Change Age" where virtually every part of business and life will be transformed. This epochal era shift is driven by the five Change Age forces: technology, globalization, information, the dismantling of hierarchy and competition. Issues Management and being ahead of the challenges and trouble will be the weapon of winners. Let's jump into the Change Age and turn on "RadarScan."

PART ONE

PLAYING IN THE FUTURE NOW

CHAPTER 1

There's No Such Thing As "On Time"

There is no such thing as "on time." There is only early and late.

If an organization waits until all the issues and forces reveal themselves and then acts, **it's always too late.** That's exactly what most organizations do because it never feels right to make a move early if the organizational culture isn't conditioned to do it. Visionary organizations develop a culture that not only accepts, but looks for harbingers that may signal a new trend or threat even when it seems implausible.

We're in the vortex of an epochal era shift, moving from the Industrial Age to the information "Change Age." Virtually every part of our lives and business will change. It's not a recession or downturn, it's a revolution in business and society. A world with out borders. An information hurricane. A technological explosion in cyberspace. And a competitive cauldron where predators stalk every company every day, waiting to pounce and attack margins. Welcome to the Change Age where issues are the bombs that destroy.

The Change Age message is that forces and trends need to be addressed **early in order to transform early.** That applies equally to RadarScan Issue Management, which is an imperative stemming from the Change Age itself and it's the same for **everyone**. No one escapes. You. Me. Large company. Small company. IBM. Jones Consulting. Everyone. Management icon Peter Drucker said it perfectly in the *Harvard Business Review,* "Every organization has to prepare for the abandonment of everything it does."

Visionary Change Age organizations mobilize people and resources to **act early....and to act now** in defining and responding to those issues which threaten survival.

Defining Issues & Issues Management

An issue can be viewed as: *an emerging internal or external force which could impact an organization's....*
- assets
- power
- image
- relationships/equity with stakeholders

- competitive position
- strategic intent
- performance
- or ability to arrive at its desired vision end state.

And an issue requires EARLY, strategic response with expectations for some degree of impact/success.

Issues Management, Then, Is...

- anticipatory readiness...an orientation to forecast and foresee...to link an organization to its world.
- an outside-in orientation and cultural mindset to open up and enhance an organization's responsiveness to change.
- an action oriented, disciplined, orderly, structured and formal framework to analyze options and alternatives before deciding on direction and action steps.
- not futurism, or reactive fire fighting in a crisis mode.
- strategic, not remedial.
- participative in public policy discourse to shape a specific issue toward the benefit of the organization and its stakeholders.
- process-oriented to identify, assess and respond to key issues, threats and opportunities in external and internal environments which will have an impact on the organization's competitive position or jeopardize relations with its stakeholders.
- focused organization-wide connection to internal/external forces filtered through the organization's vision and strategic context to see ahead and transform today in order to arrive alive tomorrow.
- information generation about strategic issues and forces and plotting their trajectories early in order to drive change and dictate the direction, scope and impact of those issues. It forces maximum results and minimizes any downside for an organization and its stakeholders.

You can see how broad the definition of an issue is, and how important it is to be on the lookout for what's coming.

Hockey superstar Wayne Gretzky inadvertently coined what is probably the most important issues management line in history when he said, "It's not where the puck is that's important, it's where it will be." There you have it, the key thing you need to know about RadarScan Issues Management in the Change Age.

A successful RadarScan Issues Management program generates data across the breadth and depth of the organization (internally and externally), makes some assumptions about the trajectories—where the puck will be—and then begins to drive the change, creating a new future through innovation.

RadarScan Issues Management In the Change Age

Why has issues management emerged as the imperative for success in the 21st century?

This issues management orientation is inextricably linked to the organization's vision and strategy. But it goes well beyond planning and instead looks for inter-relatedness. It seeks integration and a synthesis of gut feel and innovation. RadarScan Issues Management is not a planning appendage and it's not a "department."

RadarScan Issues Management is more than public relations or an image program. It's the information gatekeeper and framer. It should help people understand complex issues in an atmosphere of controversy. It means having a chance to drive an issue to its best solution consistent with the organization's goals, always balanced against the stakeholders' objectives and positions in both good and bad times.

Theodore Levitt of the Harvard Business School puts the challenge this way, "Management is about tomorrow, not today." And that's right. It's really a question of always anticipating. Always looking ahead. Always plotting the trajectory of issues and forces and doing something early to transform the area in question. This approach isn't planning based on the past. It's the opposite, always anticipating moves, trends and developments into the future...and making decisions *now* that will alter the trajectory of those issues and forces. That's "creating" a future.

Can you anticipate with complete certainty? No. Can you create a specific pathway. No. Do you need to make new assumptions and challenge old assumptions about the future and do something to transform the business? Absolutely. The focus of RadarScan Issues Management is on early involvement and getting all the facts, so informed, timely, confident strategy decisions can be made. *Early.*

The Consequences of Not Being "Early"

Example 1

Encyclopedia Britannica is a 226 year old company that survived the American Revolution. It survived the Industrial Revolution. But the venerable information giant may not make it through the Information Revolution which is exploding outside your window right now. Britannica is a classic example of waiting too long to act. The Britannica story provides an instructive lesson in what happens if you don't develop an organizational culture that embraces the notion of looking into the future and moving early. The company did finally move toward a technology-driven encyclopedia using CD-ROM, but only after its competitors had dashed out of the starting blocks and entrenched themselves in the new category. How did the company miss the mark? Britannica listened to its independent contractor sales force which was concerned that commissions on the CD-ROM disc would be less than the hard bound, 200-pound stack of books. Management buckled under the pressure.

Example 2

In 1941 an enlisted man studying his radar screen at Pearl Harbor was told by a supervisor to ignore the flock of planes that crossed his view.

Example 3

Time, Inc., the venerable publishing giant is wandering about in the Change Age looking for answers. Since its founding in 1923, *Time* Magazine has been one of the most dominant publishing forces in the world. *Time **was** America. But in the Change Age, *Time* can't find its slot in a world shifting toward electronic communication delivery. Efforts to move itself toward the needs of the younger, more electronically oriented generation, have been made without challenging assumptions about its business and the future. Critics called the moves "disastrous." Leaving behind its heritage as the preeminent news weekly, *Time* effectively turned off its core audience. After several high-profile repositioning and graphic overhauls, *Time* is still oblivious to the issues circling its multi-billion dollar fort. Is it counting on being "on time" instead of early?

Example 4

Rolodex, a name practically synonymous with card file and address products, is finding that its brand recognition doesn't mean much in the Change Age.

Competitors are stealing the show by introducing new products that mirror the exploding technological revolution. Companies like Sharp and Casio have crashed onto the scene with innovative offerings that squeezed Rolodex. This is how Rolodex management explained its predicament, "We decided to let it evolve a little bit—the whole category of personal information is too confusing." Wow! Letting issues evolve a little bit may be tantamount to signing the organization's death warrant in a world in which nothing is stable. Nothing linear. Nothing guaranteed.

"Slash & Burn"

These examples show that the most common reaction is not to "manage issues." More typically, the reaction is to "slash and burn" everything, then pass out some buttons with a new slogan and hope everything "will be okay." But slash and burn cuts eviscerate the foundation of the enterprise and carve out the ability to mount an opportunistic strike. Carve out the ability to thwart a competitor. Carve out the future and a shot at innovation. All gone. Burned to make a short-term goal.

It is no surprise, with this "on-time" mentality, management experts have demonstrated that 70 percent of change plans fail. And I'm not convinced that the other 30 percent make it. They probably aren't far enough along to know it's going to fail. These save-the-company change plans focus on incremental adjustments of current activities and not how the organization should be reoriented to identify and respond to the issues and forces it faces.

What It Means To Be Early

Example 1
Food giant Taco Bell intently watches its radar searching for emerging issues and then experiments in the marketplace to stay ahead of the Change Age monster lapping at its heels. How did Taco Bell grow from a $700 million regional player to a $3.9 billion multinational food delivery company? By reinventing the way fast food is delivered to the market and **doing it early, before all the signs were apparent.**

Taco Bell looked at the key issues driving its business into the future and then built scenarios which showed that people would eat in different ways and in different places. The innovative Taco Bell team changed the way they thought of themselves, moving from a company that prepares food to one that feeds hungry people.

Sounds pretty simple, but that future orientation— looking for the issues and forces that would determine their future success—was very powerful for Taco Bell. It led to a strategy called POA—Points of Access —any place where people can meet to eat...an airport, arena, cafeteria, college campus, or even a street corner. That shift opens up countless opportunities that simply do not exist on the conventional track which features expensive buildings scattered across the landscape just as it has always been before. The goal for Taco Bell? To increase its POAs from 15,000 to 200,000 by the year 2000.

Example 2

Crayola, the crayon icon that has been coloring the world since 1903, is one of the most recognizable brands in the world. It has reinvented itself in this era of high-tech gadgetry by always focusing ahead and thinking about the issues and forces driving its future...a passionate focus on kids and color in a never ending exploration to find what they want.

With aging baby boomers colliding with the echo baby boom, Crayola is in a sweet position demographically with an expanding target. But just being in the game means nothing for Crayola. With so many choices out there for kids toys and activities, it's no slam dunk for Crayola. After research showed that kids are always looking for coloring subjects and ideas, Crayola said it must move beyond usage per child (the average child in the U.S. will wear down 730 crayons by the age of 10) and offer something new in order to increase sales.

Enter Crayola's future-oriented view of exploring with the kids. In the last few years, Crayola has introduced a number of new items, offering new product and package sizes and broadening the possibilities of what can be done with crayons and markers. The result? Two great products—"Changeables," special wands that, with a single stroke, change the color of market drawings, and "Overwriters" which allow children to color over color, creating interesting effects. More products are on the way. Companies like Crayola are the exception. Most organizations instead opt for slash and burn cuts in order to improve their bottom line and keep the patient breathing. But cutting costs is not a sustainable strategy...and that's the irony. Most companies do need to cut back...do need to become leaner and more efficient. I've done it, and you've probably done it. But those moves must be tied to a vision for the future, to a customer and to the market. Those moves must have a contextual tie to the issues and forces shaping the game for the company.

Example 3

Computer maker Compaq has said it is gearing for "unremitting price pressure in the 21st Century where margin erosion is a given." That attitude and mindset is keeping Compaq in front of the pack as its competition drops likes flies.

Example 4

Here's an example from a small company that moved early and decisively. It's a fertilizer company in California that started from a wheel barrow three generations ago, but was being consumed by manufacturing costs and margin squeeze. The solution? Contract out the manufacturing of the fertilizer and focus on the company's strength—marketing and promotion, creating value with a customer at retail. Let other companies bid for the contract to make the fertilizer and move from cost-squeezed to the squeezer. The initial reaction from the family members of the private company? Not make the fertilizer? Blasphemy! But after a few more quarters of bleeding, the move was made and the turnaround had started. Even though the fertilizer company couldn't predict the future with precision, it could develop likely scenarios about where the company was going, and make a move toward redirection.

That's the future view. That's managing issues in the Change Age. The future view is an imperative today for all organizations even though it hasn't always been that way. In the post-war era, business grew very big as demand exceeded supply. The thirst for more was insatiable and business was relatively easy for a corporate America without competition. Prices moved inexorably upward to recover costs and maintain margin, protected from consumer resistance by the lack of competition and growing demand. But no more in the Change Age with competition lurking in every crevice.

That enlightened view is a big departure from the old world control mechanism which says, "Hey, we're protected. We're making money." "We've got a heritage." I call it the Sears mentality before its recent turnaround in the mid 1990s. "Who would ever question our position in the marketplace?" That attitude is a yellow chair.

The Yellow Chair & Transformation

Anything that prevents an organization from identifying the key issues and transforming their today in order to arrive alive tomorrow is a yellow chair. You know the story. You inherit grandma's yellow chair and begin the process of decorating around that ugly monstrosity. The initial approach commonly focuses on new carpet, paint, wallpaper and accessories. But there sits grandma's yellow chair and the room never looks right. Then the next redecorating plan. New carpet. More accessories. Still no improvement.

Finally, the old girl dies, the enlightened few lose the yellow chair and are empowered for the first time to do it right. But before they begin, everything that had been done before must be destroyed...all the carpet, all the wallpaper, all the accessories...everything...because the yellow chair had dictated everything, and ruined it all. Wasted time. Wasted money. Wasted opportunity. Irretrievable.

What's the alternative? Rather then beginning with all the furniture and accessories, **and the yellow chairs,** and then arranging...begin with a picture of the room, then gather and arrange the pieces to make your vision a reality. Every company should look for the yellow chairs that keep it from developing an anticipatory orientation to seek out the key issues and act *early*. The yellow chairs could be the lawyers. Sellers with too much influence. The shareholders. Buyers wielding unlimited power. Factions fighting and not collaborating. Outdated technology. Yellow chairs can also be key players who "own" a slot in the organization for life and will do everything to protect their turf and their position, to stifle change or innovation. Or it could be the production department's inordinate control of the sales process. Or it could be attitudes enmeshed in the culture of "we can't do that" or "we've always done it this way." The list of yellow chairs is endless, and they not infrequently show up as long-standing, impregnable assumptions.

Challenging The Assumption Trail

A great technique to move toward RadarScan Issues Management and find yellow chairs is to **Challenge the Assumption Trail.** In our RadarScan Issues Management brainstorm sessions, I display a real yellow chair on a conference table. It's a constant challenge to jump off the conventional track and reexamine traditional assumptions—those invisible premises we use to drive all strategies and tactics.

Challenging assumptions provides a fresh view into our institutionalized and most cherished ideas of the business, the products, and the competitors. It's a fresh look at all of the issues and forces through a new, *future-oriented* lens.

An illustration can be found in a recent *USA Today* article headlined "Travel Agents Train Sights on Airlines." The story chronicled how travel agents had declared war on the major airlines, some agents even going so far as calling it their "Pearl Harbor." And the attack included more than just rhetoric. Agents were booking "phantom" reservations, trying to bury the airlines in paperwork, and ordering bogus special meals. The issue? The agents were challenging a move by major airlines to cap travel agency commissions at $50.

What's going on here? Air travel is on the rise around the world. Why are the travel agents getting hit? Because the airlines are being hit. And everyone else in the economic chain is being hit with this inexorable challenge to trim costs, boost efficiency and innovate at the same time, while keeping prices down.

Remember, it's the Change Age. The travel agents, however, define their role as reservation intermediaries whose income flow comes from the airlines, hotels, and the other enterprises where they book business. You can almost feel the travel agents saying, "There's always been a need for travel agencies, and there always will be." It's that old Sears syndrome again.

Apparently they feel confident enough to mount an aggressive assault on the powerful airlines. But is that a sustainable strategy, even if they win this round? With the runaway breakthroughs in technology and everyone in business feeling the competitive needles digging into their skin, how can an "extra" and costly layer—if that's what the travel agents are becoming—survive? How can they survive when the trends say customers will use technology to communicate directly with companies like airlines, hotels and the rest?

Travel agents need to challenge their most cherished assumptions about their role in the travel industry—***and do it early***—so they can contemplate what they have to offer, then match that up with the market and the opportunities with an eye on the future. Find a niche. Create a service that transcends "taking reservations" and provides value to customers...like packaging exotic tours or cruises, or a specialized business travel service. Or? You fill in the blank.

Business is about seeing the forces and trends—"the issues"—and doing something transformative that builds value for the organization and its stakeholder ecosystem. That's why we get paid and the only way to get that huge job done is to have a fully powered RadarScan program reconnoitering on the horizon and feeding us information about issues and forces. Grasping the "on time" concept intellectually isn't enough because the game is fought in the real world by real people. As a consequence, organizing the issues management team early and strategically is essential to success in issues management. That's the focus of Chapter 2.

CHAPTER 2

Organizing For Issues Management

Traditional, linear structure doesn't work well in an amorphous, virtual environment.

When the topic of assembling an issues management team comes up, most people immediately think about public relations or communications departments. But issues management is not a "PR problem," it isn't "communications," and it isn't "relationship management," even though public relations capabilities and communication tactics do come into play in a very important way in the issues management process. Indeed, without them most issues management plans would fall flat on their faces and fail.

RadarScan Issues Management as a discipline is inextricably linked to change and strategy in the Change Age. Issues management activities transcend public relations and cut across functions as appropriate. The best approach to issues management "structure" is to move toward "Virtual Issue Teams" invested with leadership and expertise specific to the nature and scope of the issue at hand. Virtuality is another one of those "new world" business terms that has muscled its way into the lexicon, originating in the computer nomenclature as, "making a computer act as if it has more capacity."

By extension, the virtual team is a group of people positioned and enabled to act beyond their customary power, capacity and reach. The virtual issues management team subordinates overhead and permanence for scale and impact. It creates strategic configurations for quick strikes. It is a patchwork mosaic of outsiders and insiders that avoids bureaucracy through its focus, and by challenging assumptions about the issue and what can be achieved in the campaign.

Movie making and construction provide two great examples of a virtual team. People from different skill areas are thrown together on a project with the expectation that their individual and joint efforts will achieve specific goals at specific times, and with specific performance requirements. They do their jobs and when it's over, they may or may not see each other again. The virtual issues management team is a similar web of strategic resources and alliances.

Using the virtual concept, people you couldn't normally afford can be brought in for a specific issue on a tight time frame to assemble that "world class staff." With the virtual issues management approach to staffing, you can put together the

"Dream Team" with specialists from key areas that will make a difference in whether you win or lose.

Leadership on the virtual team should come from the area affected by the issue—the people with the most to gain or lose, the most passion, the most expertise, and the most connectedness on that issue. Action on issues involving government affairs may draw leadership from a government affairs department, but team members need to be drawn from all affected areas of the organization.

Connecting all issues management functions is imperative, but the connecting "home" can't be a bureaucratic cottage where issues get bogged down. It must be part of the organization's culture, with cross functional connectors coordinated by a "quarterback."

An issues management resource center is important to make sure plans are coordinated and on track. Should the home be inside the organization? What about an outside issues management agency? I believe strongly in the outside issues management agency as an adjunct to organizational efforts at building and maintaining the RadarScan Issues Management system, because building the system and analyzing inputs requires a special ability. But outside agencies can't do this alone. Everyone inside the organization participates and the outside resource makes the insiders better by providing fodder and context. The process keeps the organization challenging assumptions and reaching outside its comfort zone.

To be effective, issues management must also have top management's support and involvement starting with the CEO. The chief executive officer plays a critical role in the issues management process. The individual has to be comfortable with the RadarScan model, and has to support it enthusiastically throughout the organization. A culture must be fostered that values early detection and action, especially when the issue is a negative force or threat.

The CEO prompts the organization to probe and ask questions. He or she is intensely dedicated to fostering the organization's ability (willingness) to spot the issues and forces it to do something about them. Lacking that dedication, the solid connection to organizational vision, values, strategic frame (including the board room) required for successful issues management dissolves.

It's imperative that the issues management function have adequate financial support to more than merely watch an issue. Funding, however, often becomes a problem because issues management competes for resources with the ongoing functioning of the business. Managers from whom you are seeking resources must see that their world will be better if they are involved in addressing issues that impact them and their departments.

Developing the issues management team early is critical to success. But launching people into the issues arena without a sense of context for what the organization is and wants to be can be suicide. As discussed earlier, the Change Age is so full of challenges that finding issues to manage is not difficult. But there's not enough time or money to manage everything and time spent chasing the non-critical issues cuts directly into the organization's ability to focus on the issues that impact its future.

We've just seen how broad is the definition of issues and issues management. We've seen what it means to be early on an issue and how to organize a team to manage the response. It seems like we're all set to run, but to where? On what track? Chasing what? Part Two follows to discuss how to find those critical issues and begin development of an issues management program. It begins with Chapter 3—"Organizational Soul" the first phase in the RadarScan Issues Management Model—to determine what's important to the organization now and in the future. It discusses how to decide what road to travel with your issues management program.

PART TWO

THE RADARSCAN ISSUES MANAGEMENT MODEL

CHAPTER 3

The Organizational Soul

It may be true, as the hippie said, that everybody has to be somewhere... but soul's the secret to getting where you want to be.

We have a churning business climate producing issues in droves. And we need to anticipate where the puck will be. But before organizations can start the radar scanner, they must determine what they stand for and care about. They need to know where they want to go, and when and how they want to get there. Then they will know what issues to look for and how to respond to them. This chapter relates specifically and directly to the **"SOUL"** circle in the RadarScan Issues Management Model contained in Appendix A.

Identifying the organizational soul is the critical first step in the RadarScan Issues Management Model. An organization can't move toward issues management and transform it today in order to arrive alive tomorrow without making those efforts actionable extensions of its soul. Absent an organizational soul to serve as a rudder for identifying and managing issues, it's easy to fall into a false sense of security and "feel good" comfort zone because issues are being "monitored."

This is analogous to the myopic "strategic planning" efforts which are unaccompanied by innovation and action. Everyone feels great because there is a 300-page strategic plan on the shelf, even though nothing is "in play" to understand the issues and forces that are driving the organization.

Organizational Soul... Vision & Values

For enlightened Change Age organizations, it is becoming clear that you can't go into the marketplace and stakeholder ecosystem until you understand what you stand for. How can you deal with a safety or environmental issue when you haven't defined where you stand on that issue?

The organizational soul is the way you configure your resources, deploy your people and technology, and interact with the players in your stakeholder ecosystem. It is a way of thinking about the game. A mixture of beliefs and philosophy. Strategy and vision. The way an organization communicates. It is not detailed action steps, which represent the "how to" tactical elements of running a business.

Soul defines an organizational context, a common purpose and shared framework for action. It drives where and how we compete. How we know if we win or lose. It is the soul of the enterprise. And it's the heart of RadarScan Issues Management.

Why all of the focus on vision and soul when discussing issues management? Consider this: America won nearly every battle in the Viet Nam conflict but lost the war. There was no clear vision for victory. Is that how you are managing issues and forces? Are you fighting a Viet Nam war? Do you know what you're trying to fight? Do you know what you're trying to accomplish?

Knowing what you stand for is critical to identifying and responding to the issues and forces crashing onto the organization's beach. The way we conceive the future sculpts the present and gives tone and contour to the positions we take on the issues and forces on our radar screen in the present.

The organizational soul and context act as filters for determining the issues and forces that must be watched. But it's more than a matter of focus, it's doing the right thing. There's not enough time or money in the Change Age to deal with all the issues. And if you try, you won't handle any of them well.

That's why the soul and context must be clarified. And both are inseparable from vision. What will the market look like down the road? What will we need to do? What's needed in our products and services and processes to make that happen? What about the technology? What about the stakeholder ecosystem? What about the government? What about the competitive forces?

Vision is the map to the future, the art of the future view balanced against the day-to-day details of running a business. Think duality—operating in the present, preparing for the future. Authors Gary Hamel and C.K. Prahalad wrote in "Competing for the Future" that, on average, managers spend less than 3 percent of their time building a corporate perspective of the future. The urgent drives out the critical.

Organizations deploying a RadarScan Issues Management system should be asking the important questions such as, "How will my industry change?" "What's coming down the pike?" "Where are we at risk?" "What do we need to do about it?" "When do we need to do it?"

The Values Filter

Another element in the organizational soul is a sense of values that serves as a philosophical underpinning and filter for RadarScan Issues Management. Values are the conscience of the organization, driving management style and culture. Values provide support and security for risk taking. They provide a guide for appropriate behavior and decision making. Values are a key ingredient in the organization's soul. Values are the rudder for sound and confident issues management decisions.

The 21st century will see an explosion of the trend toward meaning-centered ethos. The growing societal complexity and intense public scrutiny pummeling all of us in the Change Age will make a "values filter" an essential part of every organization.

Johnson & Johnson has long recognized the need for a values filter. The company has a 100-year-old creed that defines what is important to the company. That creed dictates the company's actions inside and outside the organization. It is also responsible for J&J's compassionate and effective response to a crisis in the early 1980s when several people died after someone tampered with J&J's Tylenol products in the Chicago area.

J&J's crisis response to that tragedy is still considered the standard by which all others are judged. And, remember, J&J did not have a crisis response plan as so many companies do and should in today's business environment.

Remarkable! Every decision made after the poisonings came naturally as they flowed through J & J's value filter. The recall decisions, the packaging response, the statements, the hotlines, the research, everything. All solid. All without a crisis response plan.

Ben & Jerry's, the fabulous ice cream and frozen dessert company, is another great example. The culture at Ben & Jerry's embraces a cause beyond profits as it attempts to save the world from environmental destruction. And it involves the customer by donating a percentage of the profits from each purchase to well-promoted causes. In fact, many of its flavors tie back to a cause, like its "Rain Forest Delight." It buys milk for ice cream only from family farms in Vermont. It bought blueberries for one ice cream flavor from Maine's Passamaquoddy Indian tribe. And some of the profits from "Rainforest Crunch" ice cream were used to fund a nut cooperative in Brazil. Now the firm just needs to sell more ice cream.

Similarly, Starbucks Coffee of Seattle, Wall Street's darling because of its meteoric growth in the gourmet coffee craze, has a strong value filter to guide its actions and drive its marketing machine. Starbucks calls it a "Global Commitment," backed up by this statement:

> *Starbucks is North America's leading sponsor of CARE, the international aid and relief organization. The Starbucks/CARE partnership focuses on providing development and aid to people in coffee producing countries around the world.*

Projects include:
- Clean water in Guatemala and Indonesia
- Revitalization in Ethiopia
- Health and literacy in Kenya

The Starbucks creed drives how it monitors and responds to the issues and forces careening down the pike.

Many Scandinavian businesses have value filters and sell more than products. The Scandinavians actually sell values, illustrated by Volvo's success with selling safety and durability.

Another great example of the value filter in action is privately held W.L. Gore, an innovative powerhouse boasting 31 straight years of profitability. Current sales are hovering around $1 billion. Products range from Gore-Tex insulated outdoor clothing, cable insulation, vascular grafting material for surgery, industrial filters and no-stick dental floss called "Glide."

Gore's value filter plays an important role in the company's success. Its clearly stated, oft-repeated set of four core values guides all decisions on issues:
1. Fairness...a dedication to maintaining it.
2. Commitment...If you make one, you keep it. Everyone makes his or her own.
3. Freedom...The company allows individuals the freedom to grow beyond what they're doing, and they are expected to use it.

4. <u>Water line</u>...A hole above a ship's water line won't sink it, but one below it will. Certain decisions, say, building a new plant, demand consultation and agreement at Gore. Other decisions like launching a new product don't. This value substitutes for a budget.

How does the value filter get activated? Through an unflagging commitment to clear, continuous communication. And by action. By example. You can't will it, or enforce it by decree. J&J didn't win on the Tylenol issue because it had a great plan. You can't do it that way. The soul—vision and values—must run through the organization and its people through communications and actions that are interactive, genuine and continuous.

Without such a clearly defined organizational ethos, there is no context for construction of any issues management program. Clarifying the organizational soul is critical to the process of sifting through the information and finding the **strategic impact issues** facing the organization, the focus of the next chapter.

CHAPTER 4

The Issues Factory

There are better options than probable death and certain death.

There's a great tale from oil industry lore that captures the essence of our failure to respond early to issues and forces. A worker in charge of a North Sea oil rig was trained that no matter how bad any problem got, he was to wait for help. He was told **not** to jump from the 150-foot high rig into the sea **under any circumstance**. But when the rig caught fire, he jumped anyway. Asked afterward why he stepped off the edge after being told not to, he said he looked behind him and saw an approaching wall of fire...and then looked down into the icy sea...and decided to jump. "I chose probable death over certain death," he said after surviving the fall.

Eventually we all jump when the trouble is upon us, but why do we often wait until the only two choices are "probable death" and "certain death"?

The Change Age is an **issues factory** which produces bombs that, unless deflected or defused, spell probable death or certain death for organizations: a new government regulation takes your company out of a market in one fell swoop; a shift in technology leaves you flat footed and eating the dust of your nimble competitor who steals the show; a shift in demographic trends, once thought to be moving glacially slow, now explodes onto the scene and smacks your company squarely between the eyes; special interest groups camped at your door, challenging your latest project; the technology that drives your business has been totally revamped by your biggest competitor; a commodity that is integral to your manufacturing process just tripled in cost; or a foreign government is about to seize your factory.

The issues factory produces issues around the clock, every minute of every day, with potentially destructive implications for every sector of your business. Sound far fetched? Don't think it could hit you? Consider these real life examples crashing into those affected right now:

Utilities... Major utilities face a barrage of public policy trouble as we head into the 21st century. The monster issue is "Electro Magnetic Fields," but that's just the tip of the iceberg as the utilities reel under a crush of regulatory initiatives.

Balloon Makers... Tough new environmental laws threaten balloon manufacturers, as whales die on beaches after swallowing balloons, and six-ton airplane engines fail after ingesting a tiny piece of plastic.

*BBQ Lighter Fluid Manufacturers...*Urban and suburban areas are taking sight on manufacturers of lighter fluid who critics say are contributing mightily to a host of environmental problems. Makers of charcoal, in many cases the same company, aren't far behind.

*Pizza Companies That Deliver...*Pizza companies that promise delivery within 30 minutes are finding it to be a hard promise to fulfill. A rash of serious accidents involving delivery drivers has led to a flurry of legislation to outlaw the practice.

*Furniture Makers...*Environmental regulations tighten around the practices of furniture manufacturers who use petroleum-based products in their plants.

*Stock Exchanges...*A technological revolution is sweeping through the financial services business as transactions become increasingly automated. The casualty? The stodgy Exchanges which are built on tradition, paper, and CONTROL.

*Auto Mechanics...*The computerization of automobiles has revolutionized the $5 billion auto repair business. If that were not bad enough as mechanics and dealers scramble to keep up with their more technically sophisticated competitors, there's the specter of new TYPES of cars just around the corner that won't even resemble what's on the road today.

Fishermen..."Fished out" waters. High costs and low margins. A liability crisis. And toxicity levels sending many catches to the dump. Tough issues, right? Yes, but those are the OLD issues! The new threat for fisherman is coming from competitors who don't even catch their fish...they MAKE IT in a laboratory. That's right, fake fish.

That list could go on forever. The point? Everyone is affected, and it's not just the people working on the "government issues" where issues management for all practical purposes got its start. Even marketing professionals are beginning to see the need to turn the radar on so they can spot "issues." They see that success in the marketplace is impacted by issues. Most marketers stay focused on the operational part of their business. They do not get involved early and challenge assumptions, in order to spot the issues and forces that will determine their future. These organizations remain mired in the linearity of old track thinking. Extending what was instead of creating what could be.

An article on Goodyear Tire Company in the *New York Times* helps make the point. The CEO was quoted as saying, "We have to trim back and reduce our work force. We have to restructure our whole organization and make it more efficient. We have to open up new lines to countries which are blocking us politically."

Note the absence of any reference to traditional marketing problems like pricing, promotion, packaging, and competition. The challenges cited by the Goodyear CEO require issues management.

Building The Issues Factory

How did the issues factory get built? It was constructed on a foundation of five steel girders:

1) Information...it's now available to everyone, every player...customer and competitor, leveling the playing field and exposing weaknesses previously concealed by the mystique and power of companies which have been in business and dominated their territories for a long time.

2) Competition...competitors are everywhere and they are predatory to boot. At every turn someone is changing the rules, changing the balance. Cutting costs, developing new technologies, stealing customers and market share.

3) Technology...it's changing so fast no one can keep up. And automation is a requirement for entry into a market... a standard element for all organizations just to be in the game. But winning companies use their technology to go beyond automation and move toward innovation.

4) Dismantling of Hierarchy...many organizations—large and small—are shedding the rigid, centralized structures and processes that stifle innovation and bloat overhead. They are setting new standards and changing the rules for everyone. Those who don't do it find themselves in a market with nowhere to turn. Cutting the hierarchical stranglehold is an imperative, but without innovative transformation in the marketplace, and a focus on the issues, it will just be leaner inefficiency.

5) Globalization...events that once took decades to cross oceans are raining down daily and changing the dynamics in virtually every market and every sector of business. And if you don't think your product, company or industry is affected, think again. You don't have to encounter a competitive threat from off shore to be affected by this trend. Globalization allows your competitors to source cheaper components. It increases competitive pressure and lowers

margins. Globalization is really an extension of the information revolution, more players empowered by more information, producing more competition.

These five forces create an issues factory which gets its fuel from the media and information revolutions. These forces empower people, generate complexity throughout every level of society, and create issues for every business.

As societal complexity marches forward, organizations must embrace the notion of pluralism. A public policy issue that entails legitimate choices between conflicting values is not an anomaly in American democracy. Empowered publics, individuals and special interest groups create an imperative for business to recognize its place within a "stakeholder habitat." Organizations must view stakeholders (customers, shareholders, community, employees, etc.) as a vital part of the organization, but not just as "entities." They must be viewed as real people that are a part of the organization's habitat and essential for its success. Participants in the habitat include:

STAKEHOLDER HABITAT

Finance
- Security Analysts
- Portfolio Managers
- Shareholders/Investors

Government
(local, state, federal)
- Bureaucrats
- Politicians
- Regulators

Marketplace
- Customers
- Suppliers/Vendors
- The Trade
- Business Organizations
- Associations
- Allies/Competitors
- Experts/Opinion Leaders

Public Sphere
- Special Interest Groups
- Schools/Teachers
- Environmental

Media
- Regional
- National
- Special Interest
- Trade Publications

Employees
- Employee Organizations
- Labor Unions

Community
- Civic Organizations
- Religious Organizations

Threats from growing numbers of stakeholders come from differing perceptions of issue implications, and the political dynamics that result. These differences add dimensionality and velocity, intensifying the threat. Technology and a hotly competitive business arena add even more pressure. So do nearly 100,000 superbly organized special interest groups, often populated by people looking for an identity in an increasingly stratified society.

These groups are organized and shrewd, and most organizations are blind to the crippling power they can bring to issues. Their communication skills tower above those of most organizations, with powerful messages exploding on the World Wide Web, in books, news releases, events, pamphlets, direct mail, phone solicitations, and the most powerful weapon of all, television. Business, with its focus on operations (remember those yellow chairs) is commonly caught off guard, and often over matched by the special interest groups when it comes to organization and coordination.

You can't hide from critics, and if you ignore them, you do so at your own peril. Like it or not, we are all laboring in the same factory, and optimizing results requires cooperation. Bring them early into your issue management deliberations. People who feel wronged will not likely accept a proposed solution, no matter how "fair" it sounds—unless they have been involved in its development.

Organizations must be responsive to their stakeholders and build rapport and accord. Developing a two-way, symmetrical relationship will facilitate solid issues management. Each experience helps reinforce development of a culture of trust and interdependence.

Equifax, a major credit reporting service, provides a good example of accommodation. The firm expanded into direct mail marketing when that business got hot in the late 1980s. Equifax realized its database was a treasure trove and it grew quickly into a multi-million dollar business. But critics complained that the practice was violating privacy acts. Equifax had a strong basis for fighting the opposition, at least at that stage of the issue. But the company instead fell back to its own value filter which put the privacy and satisfaction of its own customers above everything.

Equifax walked away from millions of dollars and then led the move to draft a fair privacy bill in the legislature. The result? The harvesting of credit lists for direct marketing eventually became illegal and Equifax protected its franchise and core businesses. Do you think Equifax made any points with its stakeholders? Sure did. That's RadarScan Issues Management.

Other approaches miss the opportunity to engage in a discourse of mutual accommodation. No matter how hard you work on an issue or how much money you spend, if the solution fails to be a win-win accord embracing stakeholder needs, it will always fall short of optimum performance, leaving you somewhere between probable death and certain death.

Spending time at the issues factory and knowing what fuels it are critical to success in issues management. Knowing who's living in the stakeholder habitat near the factory is also an imperative. But knowing how to position the organizational scanner and what to look for coming out of the factory is just as important. All issues aren't created equal and that's the focus of Chapter 5.

CHAPTER 5

Turning on the Radar Scanner

People may be created equal, but information is NOT.

Even though many of the RadarScan Issues Management activities are being carried out across corporate America, they're being done in many cases without an organized system. It's just like marketing before it became a multi-disciplined process. Companies were performing the various activities, but they weren't recognized as parts of an integrated whole working together. It's the same right now for issues management.

The challenge is to build an integrated framework for issues management, which leads to development of options for response or non-response to issues. The goal is to get into the anticipatory mode, looking for "where the puck will be," and staying out of the crisis response orientation. The key is to gain control of the issue early to diffuse its force or reorient its path.

But most organizations don't do that. They more typically fall into a pattern of waiting and hoping the issue will go away. Many even deny the issue exists. The rarer organizations, however, are the ones that respond to and drive issues.

They tend to survive and thrive by using their resources to direct and leverage change by acting early and experimenting. Like Crayola on the business side of the spectrum, it's a matter of recognizing shifts, trends, and marketplace dynamics in order to respond early. Smart managers don't wait for a crisis or the bomb to land. They seek and uncover, engage and adjust.

This chapter describes some of the tools required to survive and thrive in the Change Age, and relates specifically to the **"SCAN"** circle of the RadarScan Issues Management Model in Appendix A.

One of the great equalizers in the Change Age is that with minimal hardware and software investment, any organization—from a Fortune 500 firm to a one-person consultancy—has access to the same information. The potential downside is that you have to know what to look for, how to find it, and what to do with it. The difficulty, most frequently, is in separating the important from the trivial. Because information overload is always a danger, with the potential for undermining the issues management process, it becomes necessary to carefully focus on and seek out those sources most likely to contain information relevant to your needs.

Successful RadarScan Issues Management involves specifying information resources to be tapped, who will be responsible for monitoring them, how frequently, how and to whom results will be communicated, and who will prioritize issues and according to what criteria. If you're not "brailling your world" in this way, on a macro and micro level, you've already lost.

On every issue, there is always a point of incipience. Ideas don't just show up in *USA Today* or even in your industry's trade publication. They evolve through a subtle, incremental process formed and driven by opinion leaders, including those special interest groups discussed earlier. Issues often begin in obscure publications—journals, conference speeches and panels—then are increasingly picked up by mainstream mass media, becoming a part of the political agenda. The RadarScan system must be operational before issues emerge as part of the general public discourse, while the clay is still wet and you can make a difference.

There is a need for information from two areas: macroenvironmental trend data on the broad picture surrounding and involving the organization, and information from the organization's internal world. The scanner's field of view should include the following areas of potential impact:
- Economics
- Labor
- Domestic & global competition
- Technological shifts
- Supplier relationships
- Politics & government
- Public interest groups
- Social shifts
- Media content
- Marketplace changes

Environmental Scanning & Information
Here are the scanning tools available to issues managers:
- News Sources and Consultants
  — Yankelovich Partners and similar firms
  — Nexus
  — Dow Jones News/Retrieval
  — Data Times

- — View text
- — Specialized trade media, domestic and foreign mass media *(The Asian Wall Street Journal, the Financial Times, or Die Neue Zurcher Zeitung* will often carry stories that signal competitive moves.)
- — Journals/scientific papers
- — On-line wire services
- Government Reports
  - — Legislative reports
  - — Hearings
  - — Committee reports
  - — Federal/State government leadership reports
- Formal Research
  - — General
  - — Specific
- Competition
  - — Annual reports
  - — Newsletters
- Organization
  - — Employees
  - — Customer contact
  - — Volunteers
  - — Vendors/suppliers
- Public
  - — Public opinion network
  - — Focus groups
  - — Polls/surveys
  - — Experts, allies, authorities, advocates
- Computer searches/analyses
- Industry
  - — Trade shows/conventions/conferences
  - — Association reports
  - — Issue experts
  - — Newsletters
- Professional meetings
- Advisory Councils
- Anecdotal
- Legal

The traditional approach includes anything published: newspapers and magazines, trade journals, newsletters, government and court documents, company reports, investment and financial publications. This group also includes on-line databases and the Internet.

Public data are another traditional resource that most executives dismiss because they're not "exclusive." But if you want to understand your competitor's problems, look at the analyst reports from the brokerage houses. The largest financial firms publish more than 1,800 reports each year. Study your competitors' communications. Develop a system to monitor their published statements, house organs, public reports, speeches, and advertisements. The non-traditional approach focuses more on a human perspective and consists of direct observations and interviews with employees, former employees, suppliers, distributors, and customers. You can also call credit rating services, advertising agencies, analysts, and authors of articles and reports to get insights.

The best intelligence doesn't always come from costly databases. Experts say that between 70 percent and 80 percent of what businesses need to know is already known by somebody in-house. The goal is to find the person who has the information you need. That's why every person associated with the organization—inside and out—should be an "information scout" with an inquisitive nature and the freedom to uncover bad news. We should develop a culture that values a healthy outward focus.

A large amount of solid information comes from unexpected sources, in unexpected situations. The employees in the trenches are the people with the access on a regular basis to the rocks that contain gold. Use "soft soundings" to gather personalized intelligence. Soft soundings are informal chats about a specific issue. Even though they are not "projectable" in a statistical sense, they can still give you a "feel" for an issue. Ask questions, probe and explore to uncover the gold nuggets.

Employees and the teams that they participate on can also encourage suppliers and other "outside" stakeholders to supply information on issues. This is a fertile area for real information not bound by fear of job security or reprimand. Questionnaires internally and externally provide solid snapshots of what's happening, especially if the questions probe for the trouble spots and go beyond today to look at what tomorrow may bring.

Traditional or non-traditional, don't overlook your own information. Take a look at what you **already have**. All of us are guilty here. Expensive research studies sit untouched because they are seemingly amorphous or "too difficult to understand or too abstract to apply." The Japanese and Koreans are considerably more assiduous in their quest for data, its manipulation and analysis. We should develop a formalized system to make sure it gets done.

Scanning Identified Resources

Setting up the scanner system requires being sensitive to what we "need to know," not what would be "nice to know." We need to determine which areas present a threat to our competitive balance, the STRATEGIC IMPACT ISSUES. Which areas are hiding bombs that, if dropped, will sink the organization's ship? *That focus is imperative because every issue looks like a bomb. But the pertinent question is "will it sink the ship?" Will it put you out of business? That's the Strategic Impact Test.*

Few organizations, however, have the resources to properly address more than three critical issues at a time. We need to develop the filter and criteria that constitute the Strategic Impact Test, to find the bombs that might "sink the ship," and these criteria may vary from business to business, industry to industry. Specifying them, however, is critical to sorting out the strategic impacts and prioritizing the issues.

The prioritization takes on a graphic character when issues are placed in what I call the "FOCUS RING." Here, issues are displayed in three concentric rings, three issues per ring, with strategic impact issues occupying the inner-most ring (ring 1), critical issues the next (ring 2) and issues that bear watching the outer-most ring (ring 3).

Remember, only those issues passing the STRATEGIC IMPACT TEST are candidates for ring 1. If the issue fails to pass the test, it is relegated to either ring 2 or 3. Which of those two rings is most appropriate is largely a function of issue imminence and estimated issue impact, when and if the issue matures.

The objective is to identify those strategic impact issues that will put you out of business, those issues that would enhance your business, and those in between.

The key is to agree on what is critical, and then amass sufficient resources to respond, moving methodically through a prioritized list of objectives and issues.

The Tactical Response System

Identify individuals responsible for staying in touch with assigned resources relevant to their areas of expertise, and participating in a formalized reporting, evaluating and prioritizing process. Organizations should give their information scouts incentive to find trouble. The bigger the impact or scope, the bigger the reward. A RadarScan "Issue Alert" form should be developed so people can feed information into the system, taking into account the Strategic Impact Test, which, simply stated, is this:

Will the issue, if it comes to full fruition and is left unattended, be the bomb, or among the bombs, that could sink the ship and organization?

Another effective tool to use in the formal input channel is an "Advice Squad" of outside advisors. More than a board of directors, an advice squad is a collection of resources which represents the key aspects of the business to help the organization man the radar screen.

At the Avocado Commission, we have a nutrition advice squad which meets annually. The group discusses macro trends in nutrition and the specific issues affecting avocados, things like perceptions on healthfulness, calories and fat. The squad is made up of respected academicians and nutrition specialists from the top universities in the U.S. Each session produces new insights into the nutrition world and the positioning of avocados.

Forming an advice squad pays off beyond the information generated at the sessions. It also puts a leadership halo above the sponsoring company. If your company is in robotics, you could organize and conduct a symposium on "Robotics and Technology in the 21st Century." This plan lends itself well to turning the radar screen on to see the future NOW. Who would participate? Scientists. Consultants. Futurists. Writers from the leading trade publications. Customers. Special interest group leaders. Academia. Researchers. Stakeholders. You get the idea.

The same model works for insurance, construction, food, manufacturing, transportation, agriculture, telecommunications, retailing, aerospace, computers...you name it. You can pay the group, but watch out for creation of a de facto board with all the turf troubles and "yes man" weaknesses inherent in a conventional board of directors.

The goal is simple. Open up your organization to new, fresh input that challenges assumptions about where the organization is and where it needs to go in the future in order to openly scan for the Strategic Impact Issues. Over time, your organization will become adept at spotting the critical issues on the scanner. But that's just one important step. Then the hard work starts as you dig into those critical issues in order to assess them for probability, impact and risk. That tough task is explained in the next chapter.

CHAPTER 6

The Analysis Factor

Everything is composed of relationships...and they are always more convoluted than you thought they were.

Even though the scanner has been focused and is filtering out the non-strategic issues, we're still faced with the need to **do something** with the information on the issues that pass the Strategic Impact Test. This chapter is related to the **"ANALYZE"** circle of the RadarScan Issue Management Model in Appendix A. It's the analytical phase of RadarScan Issues Management in which data are manipulated and reconfigured to determine what action, if any, should be taken.

The challenge is to imbue the data with meaning because information by itself is useless. It must be contextualized and dimensionalized against the organization's strategic direction in order to configure it in a way that provides a **practical pathway for action**. Doing something with an expectation of success and impact!

This is a detailed, expensive and time-consuming phase, and considerable restraint is required to keep the number of issues well within the parameters of the focus ring discussed earlier. If an organization does a good job of crystallizing its strategic focus and vision/values soul...and directs the scanner properly, it increases its chances of avoiding mistakes made by overloading its analytical resources. The model that follows works for a multi-billion dollar issue, as well as a small competitive threat sketched out on a napkin at lunch.

All issues go through a life cycle, passing through several phases. It's important to determine early which phase the issue currently is in and evaluate its likely progression.

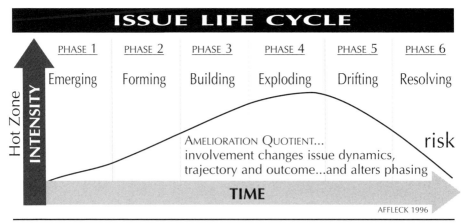

ISSUE LIFE CYCLE

PHASE 1	PHASE 2	PHASE 3	PHASE 4	PHASE 5	PHASE 6
Emerging	Forming	Building	Exploding	Drifting	Resolving

Hot Zone

INTENSITY

AMELIORATION QUOTIENT...
involvement changes issue dynamics,
trajectory and outcome...and alters phasing

risk

TIME

AFFLECK 1996

The Issue Life Cycle

The Issue Life Cycle
1. Emerging - Issue begins to appear in academic literature, at conferences, trade shows, competition literature, and trade publications.
2. Forming - Issue begins to take form. Position staked out. Analytical weight added. Groups take sides.
3. Building - Issue takes on movement and force, momentum builds.
4. Exploding - Issue reaches zenith and pops open. Critical juncture in which way it will be resolved.
5. Drifting - Issue has crested and begins to settle onto its final pathway, may continue forming as it drifts.
6. Resolving - Issue resolution.

Analysis Tools

Analyzing issues, in the end, is an art. The issue manager must become the artist and paint the canvas with the right combination of analytical methods, quantitative and otherwise. What follows is the array of brushes available for that job:
1. Scenario Building - Take the issue and play out a scenario or scenarios as to what will/could happen.
2. Trend Extrapolation - Extend a trend out over time.
3. Technological Forecasting - Use computer technology to forecast possible pathways quantitatively.
4. Decision Analysis - Play out a decision and what it would create.
5. Precursor Analysis - What will/could it lead to? Review various "ends" the issue could create.
6. Delphi Feedback - Information frame sent to a group of people who provide input and send it back. New master created and sent back to group, and so on.
7. Focus Groups - Small roundtable discussions on a specific issue, led by a facilitator.
8. Scan Session Brainstorming - Cross functional team develops shared understanding of different views on an issue and how the pieces fit together to make a whole.

9. <u>Trajectory Projection</u> - "Backcasting" reviews a previous period, using the past to chart direction and velocity for the future. This process avoids surprises where the issue seems to be crawling along glacially, but over time those incremental changes collectively add up to major impact and power.

10. <u>Force Field</u> - Social psychologist Kurt Lewin developed the notion of a force field to describe his view of the *interrelatedness* of psychological and social influences. His force field model involves deep questioning on:
    - How can we minimize the roadblocks?
    - What's working in our favor?
    - How can we strengthen those forces?
    - What can we do to move the issue in our direction?

    I use "force field" to determine what obstacles can be removed and how all of the relevant influences interact and impact the construction of my response on the issue.

11. <u>Media Analysis</u> - Dig beyond the "headlines" and go deeper into the content of collected media coverage. The results augment public opinion research because they go beyond what issues people are thinking about, and move toward how they are behaving on those issues. News can be sorted in "favorable" and "unfavorable" categories, and computer software is available to assist in the analysis. The more articles, the better the analysis. And the longer the period they cover, the better, because shifts, dynamics and patterns begin to appear over time.

Having taken the available information and data and used the analytical tools to determine its shape and scope, it's time to assess the issue's **PROBABILITY, IMPACT** and **RISK**. Most issues management efforts fly quickly through the latest information and focus on the most apparent impacts and risks. Upon closer evaluation, many items thought to be the most troublesome can actually fall subordinate to others. That's why it's critical on EVERY ISSUE to go through a methodical and organized effort to assess probability, impact and risk.

It's like a pilot getting ready for his flight by checking the aircraft before EVERY flight, just to be sure everything is covered and nothing overlooked. It's the same for issues management efforts. We should go through a formal process of evaluating probability, risk and impact for every issue. Using this approach will help ensure that all areas were considered and, importantly, all relevant information was prioritized and assessed relative to all the other parts. What follows is the RadarScan Issues Management Probability-Impact-Risk-Assessment worksheet.

Probability - Impact - Risk Assessment

- IMPACT
  - What will it be?_____
  - How will it happen?_____
  - When will it happen?_____
  - Short term/long term?_____

- PROSPECTS FOR SUCCESS
  - What can we do about it?_____
  - Can we influence it?_____
  - Should we influence it?_____
  - What's the best case victory?_____
  - What's the medium case victory?_____
  - What's the worst case victory?_____
  - Likelihood of prevailing?_____

- FORCE/VELOCITY
  - Momentum factor?_____
  - Will it escalate?_____
  - Does it have explosion/crisis potential?_____
  - Will it fizzle out (short life)?_____
  - Will it have legs (long life)?_____

- PROBABILITY
  - Will it go away on its own?_____
  - What happens if we ignore it?_____
  - What happens if we go half-way?_____
  - What happens if we go hard?_____

- RISK / VULNERABILITY
  - Does it impact/endanger any of the organizational "tent poles"?_____
  - Business loss/disruption?_____
  - Assets at risk?_____
  - Quantify downside risk_____
  - Quantify upside potential_____

Image?_____

Negative publicity?_____

Public opinion unrest?_____

Customers?_____

Marketplace?_____

Competitive position?_____

- DATA

  Is there enough available?_____

- MEDIA

  Interest in issue?_____

  Victim/culprit?_____

  Exposure?_____

  Duration?_____

  Where is the issue on the emotion meter?_____

  How will media "play it"? Will it take sides?_____

  Which media?_____

- PUBLIC

  Degree of entrenchment?_____

  Changeable?_____

- OPPONENTS/ALLIES

  Strength/size of opponents/advocates?_____

  What will be their position?_____

  What will they do?_____

  Are there allies/coalition candidates?_____

  Would they get involved?_____

  Who is fulcrum player/leader; who drives/decides issue?_____

  Who are adversaries?_____

  Actions to date?_____

- TIMING

  Positives of going out early?_____

  Risk of waiting?_____

- STRATEGY/SOUL
    Isolation of organization's position?_____

- GEOGRAPHICAL IMPLICATIONS?_____

- RESOURCES
    To act?_____
    To win?_____

- STAKEHOLDER IMPACT ANALYSIS
    Primary_____
    Secondary_____
    Tertiary_____
    Peripheral_____
    Behavioral inclinations_____
    How do stakeholders view organization position?_____

- LEGISLATIVE/REGULATORY IMPLICATIONS?
    _____
    _____
    _____

- LEGAL IMPLICATIONS?
    _____
    _____
    _____

- INTENSITY
    1. Fire - (smother)_____
    2. Hot - (get involved)_____
    3. Warm - (monitor)_____
    4. Cool - (abandon)_____

- SPECIAL CONSIDERATIONS?
    _____
    _____
    _____

Sizing Up The Target

After gaining a sense for the impacts, probabilities, and risk, developing a clear profile of the stakeholders involved in a particular issue must be a central analytic objective. Take into account anyone whose **behavior** you seek to change or reinforce. What individuals, groups, and institutions may perceive their core values, health, economics or security to be threatened by the issue?

The profile will always involve two broad classes of stakeholders, those internal to the organization and those external to it. In both cases, it is necessary to define as precisely as possible the characteristics of both groups with regard to:

- Demographics
  - Age
  - Income
  - Sex
  - Education
  - Family
  - Ethnicity/Race
- Psychographics
  - How does the stakeholder think?
  - What are the stakeholder's self-perception, values, and world view?
  - Develop a "Personality Profiles" matrix on the stakeholder(s).
  - Start with core values, what they care about, where they are now in life— security, stability, finances, politics, family, etc.—and where they are headed into the 21st century.
- Lifestyle
- Attitudes
  - Place stakeholder on "attitude and opinion continuum" from hard-core adversaries to alignment with your position. This exercise yields important information because those "on the bubble" are generally open to reformation of attitudes and can frequently be changed.
- Beliefs
- Behavior
  - What is the stakeholder's existing position?
  - What is the stakeholder's existing behavior?
- Perceptions
  - What is the reality vs. the perception?

- Can we bridge the "Perception Chasm," even with the best program, ideal situation, lots of money and everything in perfect alignment?
- Why should the stakeholder care about us—rationally and emotionally?
- What's "in it for the stakeholder" to give us what we want?
- How can we show the stakeholder we care about the same things and build rapport?
- Can we create a "swinging gate" to let each side into the other's "yard" for two-way, interactive communication and acceptable resolution?
- Will the stakeholder reject us as a sender of messages in the future because of this attempt to change/reinforce his/her behavior?

- Power
  - How capable is the stakeholder?
  - Where does it get its power?
  - Who influences the stakeholder on this issue?
  - Where does the stakeholder get its information on this issue?
  - What is the group's credibility factor?

Issue Summary

After completing the Probability/Impact/Risk Assessment and "Sizing Up The Stakeholder," develop your own "scorecard" via your Issue Summary. Transferring the information to a spreadsheet matrix may help, but I've found that issues rarely lend themselves to precision when it comes to assessing probability, impact and risk. In fact, a more likely scenario is using gut intuition after going through the more formalized exercises of asking and answering the questions above.

A useful starting point in development of the scorecard is to construct a tight summary to analyze the issue and your response options. The summary should be clear and concise. It will become a useful tool for briefings, internal communications, and planning. Include the following:

- Background of Issue
  —Origin/Source
  —Path to date
  —Previous experience on issue
  —Issue leader/ownership/team members
  —Stakeholder(s)

- Where the Issue is in its Life Cycle
  - — Emerging
  - — Forming
  - — Building
  - — Exploding
  - — Drifting
  - — Resolving
- Organization Position
- Primary Message Array (This will be explained in the next chapter.)
- Driving Forces/Restraining Forces
- Future Projections/Trajectories
- Implications/Risk
- Resources Required (General)
  - — specific budget implications later after strategies developed
- Internal Communication Plan
- External Spokesperson
- Toughest Question to Answer?
- Opportunity for Dialog with Opposition?
- Options?
- Timing?
- Decision?

Issue Mapping

Following the Probability Impact Risk Assessment and Issue Summary, map the issue graphically to depict the component interrelatedness and connectedness. This exercise clarifies the dynamics and makes the forces come alive. Build in assumptions, project evolutionary milestones, trajectories, impacts and the other key elements that have emerged from your analysis. Use the picture/map to be a visual catalyst for strategy and action.

The key to issue mapping is simplicity and creativity. There are no rules or guidelines. Just map out the issue and its key parts in order to create a visual sense of the individual parts making up a cohesive whole. The beginning point should be whenever an event becomes critical to the overall issue. For some issues that go years back, you will need to choose the point that provides context to the issue's path and present status. The end point will always adjust to the most recent events.

We created an issue map for the Mexican avocado issue and it helped us watch the issue's development and see the big picture in the middle of an intense and fast-moving fight. Take a look at it below.

The issue map is a great way to summarize the issue's components and the completed analysis. It is a perfect trigger point for the development of strategies and tactics. This is a critical juncture because so much work has been done up to this point on contextualizing the issue and preparing the organization for the battle. But you don't effectively manage issues with a great analysis and pretty poster. The battles are won in the trenches with solid, well-executed strategic action plans. Building that "Strategic Frame" is the focus of Chapter 7.

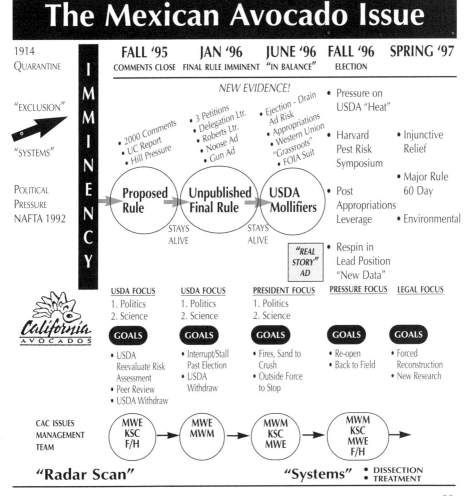

PART THREE

BEGIN TO BEGIN ...TAKE ACTION!

CHAPTER 7

The Strategic Frame

It's a lot more like skeet shooting than firing at still targets; everything has a distressing tendency to keep moving.

We understand the issue, we're sensitive to the direction dictated by our values and vision, we've specified the broad, organizational goals, and we're ready to move. The first step at this point is to define in **measurable** terms the micro-level goals to be achieved in addressing the issue at hand. This is critical to subsequent evaluation, and the failure to do so haunts many issue management projects, sometimes resulting in tragic mistakes. This chapter relates to the **"STRATEGY"** circle in the RadarScan Issues Management Model, shown in Appendix A.

The specification of issue-oriented goals necessarily involves assessing response options, taking into account human and financial resources. What is possible? What is achievable? What is affordable?

RadarScan Issues Management goals should avoid an "us against them" focus where the thrust is to "beat the other side." Winning may not be a victory. Indeed, it probably isn't, unless other stakeholders also win. The goals ought to focus on minimizing the downside and maximizing the upside.

This is one of the biggest misconceptions surrounding issues management— that the goal is always to "win and make the issue go away." The real goal is to minimize the downside, or leverage the issue to its maximum positive end while working with all parties involved to create win-win scenarios, creating balance more favorable to the organization. As a consequence, it's important to decide during goal-setting what "winning" means.

Obliterating the opposition and ripping its fabric to shreds can carry huge risks. The losing side can become a victim or martyr if the victory is overpowering. The media and public love stories about the "victim." Avoid "killing" the other side and realize it is part of your stakeholder habitat and here to stay. Inherent in the RadarScan Issues Management model is a degree of compromise. No organization can completely change and dictate public opinion in any case, even though most organizations want to and many try.

Moving toward a win-win, outside-in orientation carries with it the need to control optimism and expectations internally during the goal-setting phase.

Avoid over-promising things you can't deliver because it sets up a "failure" if things don't reach that idealized outcome. You'll have to battle the internal pressure to "cream the other side." But it will pay off when expectations are under control early during goal-setting so the organization can focus on injecting itself into the debate in a responsible way. When expectations are controlled, the strategies and tactics are frequently more realistic and measured, with less emotionalism and risk.

Keep in mind during goal-setting that...***what might have been reasonably expected to happen or be said, that didn't happen or wasn't said, may be a critical part of the analysis, spelling the difference between program success and failure.***

The last step in the goal-setting process is to pass them through your ***values filter***. This is critical because on tough issues—environmental, safety, financial, or just about anything sensitive—you may be tempted to move in a way that isn't consonant with your VALUES FILTER or the best interests of those in your STAKE-HOLDER HABITAT. It's a good idea to ask these questions before you make a move:
1. Is our position and the behavior we seek ethical?
2. Is our approach ethical?
3. If everyone could see all of our thoughts and plans, would they pass the integrity test? Are we sure?

As you develop the issue strategy, it's imperative to make sure that enough resources are available to put the chosen strategy "in play." From where will they come? What about a contingency if things accelerate beyond projections and the organization needs to mount an unplanned, and unbudgeted attack?

Resource analysis and budgeting are dealt with in greater detail later, but at this stage we should start to size up the challenge and think of the general resources required to wage the fight. It's a simple test. If you can't sustain it, don't go. If you're not prepared for exigent circumstances, don't go. Don't even try. Another key question is whether or not the strategies you are considering will make an impact and achieve the goals established. Are they enough? Are you sure?

This is another big mistake made by issue managers, working furiously on the mechanics but never putting anything "in play" that will transform the issue. It reminds me of the lessons I've learned fishing for blue marlin off the Kona Coast in Hawaii. The most successful approach is to use live, six-pound AKU tuna as bait in the "hunt" for blues. The small fish are caught with light tackle and carefully handled to insert the line and hook through their gills before tossing them back into the water. The bait then swims along freely with the four-inch marlin hook dangling from its mouth. The marlin sees the tuna swimming and strikes.

The entire process is obviously contingent on finding and catching the bait. It's not uncommon to go a few hours searching unsuccessfully for bait. During the chase for bait, you know you have nothing in play and have no chance at the marlin even though live-bait fishing is a proven method and you're a "great fisherman." When you have trouble finding bait, you ask yourself at what point do you abandon efforts to fish with live bait and instead toss the artificial lures into the water? After two hours of searching for bait, it's a tough question to answer.

It's the same for Issues Management. At some point, you must decide how you'll address the issue, and then construct your response through a communication program. And in the final analysis, it's all about persuasion and winning the game of moving all stakeholders to the strategic spot you've established. The next chapter looks this idea of a "Persuasion Purpose" and how to mount your campaign.

CHAPTER 8

The Persuasion Purpose

You've succeeded if, at the end, they believe they won.

This chapter relates to the **"ACTION"** circle in the RadarScan Issue Management Model, and is concerned, among other things, with:

- Persuasion Pathway & Processing
- Method of Dissemination
- Method of Reception
- Recipient Retention
- Message Timing
- Stakeholder Beliefs
- Stakeholder Attitudes
- Stakeholder Behaviors

At the outset, it bears noting that an effective issues management response program never generates only a single response by the organization mounting an issues management campaign. Responses are always plural, dictated by the different categories within the audience array. Effective persuasion requires producing messages appropriate to internal and external audiences, which can each be subdivided into those who agree with you, those who oppose you, and those who are neutral. Beyond messages, each of the six groups may require different information conduits. Ways of effectively transmitting information inside your own house probably will not work with stakeholders located on the outside.

Persuasion

By and large, whatever the nature of your responses, they will have a fundamentally **"PERSUASIVE PURPOSE."** It is crucially important, however, to determine who needs to be persuaded of what—and, indeed, whether or not certain stakeholders are persuadable. Internal stakeholders may agree with you, disagree with you or remain neutral for reasons utterly unlike those motivating the external stakeholders.

Communication developed for those who agree with you needs to be reinforcing, persuading group members that siding with you remains the right thing to do. This is relatively easy to achieve because you are preaching to the choir.

For those who are neutral, communication needs to be directed at moving them to your side of the fence, giving them reasons to, at minimum, agree with you, and, best case scenario, actively support you. With opponents, two courses of action are open: ignore them, because proselytization is unlikely, or provide them with sufficient information of a sort to mitigate their active opposition.

It's important to take into account, as well, the matter of communication elaboration. How will the information be processed when it is received? Generally, those opposed to your position will pay pretty close attention to what is being said, and process the information rigorously and critically. The same may well be true of those who are neutral. Those already sharing your coffee and campfire, however, are less likely to invest a lot of time and effort in critical information processing.

Messages and channels of dissemination need to be selected with these differences in mind. Your purpose, for example, may be best served using visual messages for those already in your camp, and more durable, written messages for neutrals, whose conversion may require more intensive message processing. In all cases, receptivity to the organization's message depends on the sincerity and quality of ideas, and, critically, the degree to which proposed solutions or actions take into account the other side, its position and its interests.

Remember, the stakeholder probably . . .
- doesn't understand the issue.
- doesn't care about your organization or your message.
- won't elaborate fully on your communication.
- won't follow your plan to the letter.
- is suspicious of you and your message.

Stakeholders will always respond more favorably when the appeal is framed in their self interest. This approach also has the advantage of forcing you to think of the issue and its resolution in long-range terms. Clean-it-up-fast campaigns rarely work. Moreover, in general, highly emotional, firmly entrenched issues require longer resolution periods. Move deliberately and patiently, working from a solid, substantive position, with a genuine commitment to maintaining a dialog with the involved stakeholders over time.

Whatever response is constructed, its implementation is fundamentally a matter of persuading other stakeholders to see the issue and your proposed solutions as consonant with their self interests, and to buy in. The best way to achieve that is to provide information which will encourage self persuasion, a conviction that they are better served supporting you—or, at minimum, remaining neutral—than they are opposing you.

When it comes to putting the strategy in play, the focus should be on getting beyond the mechanics of audience reach and penetration, and moving toward understanding and connecting with the audience to *affect its behavior*. First, however, a cautionary note.

The Logic Myth

Most organizations are so convinced they are "right" that they slam into the audience with their logic and then stand back incredulously and wonder why the stakeholder "doesn't understand." It's really a simple and basic communication phenomenon: Truth is a highly subjective phenomenon, and your logic—as solid as it may be—may not be received, elaborated on, processed, and accepted.

We should put our position and messages through the stakeholder's *perspective filter*. Different stakeholders have different perspectives and they approach issues from different angles, guided by demographic, psychographic and other variables already discussed. Influencing the stakeholder requires messages and actions that connect with their perspective and the things they care about. The communication must raise and focus on a need, concern or interest of the stakeholder.

The consequences of leaving the issue unresolved must be clear, along with your role or solution, but *always* from their world view and specific perspective. Words by themselves won't do it in any case. There must be substance and genuine action toward a win-win outcome. Moving in this direction toward an audience-focused, behavioral orientation requires some knowledge of stakeholders' *belief bases* and *attitudes*, which drive *behavior*.

What belief base and attitudes does a stakeholder have to hold to precipitate a move toward the attitudes and behaviors the organization seeks? What must the *stakeholder think, believe and feel*, in order to *act*? And, consistent with belief bases, attitudes and desired behaviors, what information does the stakeholder need? What information will be deemed salient or relevant? What themes, symbols, or visuals extending from the stakeholder's core values would break through the clutter, stimulate emotive responses and produce a willingness to process the information?

Breaking Through The Clutter

Once the target analysis is complete, it's time to move toward message construction. Making that job tough is the Change Age and its companion, the Information Revolution, which have produced a torrent of communications. The resulting "noise" makes it difficult for even the most sophisticated communicators.

Breaking through that clutter requires a special kind of creativity. Creatively produced messages get people to take a look at the communication and elaborate on it. Without that, we don't have a chance of persuading anyone. I've found that creativity in issues management is **less** about pretty pictures and expensive printing, and **more** about moving away from convention and pedestrian persuasion pathways.

The Persuasion Pathway

People receiving messages process them through a pathway including several steps, most of them in the subconscious part of the mind. Communicators trying to persuade a stakeholder need to understand that process and then construct their messages with it mind. Here is the persuasion pathway:

- Message Reception - *communication lands*; obvious need to be arresting, to break through the clutter in an intrusive way.
- Message Processing - *communication processed and put in a general category*; simplicity is important here so there is immediate understanding.
- Message Retention - *communication retained or drifts off*; persuasion is won or lost here. Did the message remain in the receiver's mind or was it wasted?
- Beliefs Reformation/Modification - *beliefs adjusted* (if appropriate); you're over the hump if communication reaches this stage. Again, simplicity is the key in order to have the stakeholder focus on something very specific.
- Attitudes Reformation/Modification- *attitudes* (a bundling of the beliefs) *adjusted* (if appropriate); by now receiver is doing all of the work and moving toward a behavioral change.
- Behavior/Action - ultimate action step by receiver taken.

Simple & Strategic Messages

Another key point in optimizing persuasion power is simple and strategic message construction that will affect the stakeholder's behavior and change the balance toward you and your goals. Messages must be crystal clear, concise and to the point. Key messages must be clear and powerful. The more direct and specific your communication, the better your chances of impact.

In order to construct simple and strategic messages, discipline yourself to focus on a "Primary Message Array (PMA)." The PMA may carry a long list of support stories, facts and examples, but the platform message must be clear and never comprised by other messages. In addition to the impact a PMA has with the stakeholder, the media's tendency to work tirelessly to find holes and inconsistencies is strong incentive to keep the position strong and simple and *never* move off your PMA.

In addition to simplicity and clarity, the message must be repeatedly hammered home. The more direct and specific your communication, the better your chances of impact. Help the stakeholder *visualize* and mentally conceptualize the action you would like taken.

Persuasive messages usually contain one of these three elements (or some combination):
- Rational and factual frame
- Emotionally driven, value-based element
- Sexy packaging, hook

Message Delivery

After the PMA is established, it's time to consider message delivery. Review the following considerations:
- What should be the timing and pace of message delivery?
- What channels—national, regional and local—are appropriate?
- How much emphasis should be placed on each channel?
- What should be the timing and pace of message delivery through each channel?
- Which communication vehicles are most appropriate for which audiences?
  — Advertising
  — Publicity
  — Speech Platforms

- — Telemarketing/800 lines
- — Face-to-Face Personal Visits
- — Film
- — Video
- — Special Events
- — Contributions
- — Small Group Participation and Networking
- — Exhibits
- Which media?
  - — TV
  - — Radio
  - — Internet
  - — Outdoor
  - — Direct
  - — Print
- What trajectory would the communication take and how long before it would be effective?
- When is the best time to execute this strategy?
- Is that the only window of opportunity?
- What happens if you miss it?
- What must you do to assure that you won't miss it?
- What is the timeline for communication?
- Are there differences between internal and external communications?
- Does the strategy encourage two-way communication?
- Will your actions be viewed as credible from the stakeholder's perspective?
- What level of consent is required of the stakeholder?
- What type of participation from the stakeholder is required? Possible?
- How will the stakeholder's reactions be identified, analyzed, and addressed?
- How will continuous feedback from the stakeholder be assured?
- How will risks and uncertainties be explained to the stakeholder?
- How will organization credibility be checked throughout the action?

Look at the above list as a guide. Don't overcomplicate the process by laboring over a sea of details and possibilities. The key is getting something "in play." Most issue managers think too much here and try to make the program sweeping and fancy. Remember, it comes down to persuasion. Know what your message is and develop a Primary Message Array. Understand your stakeholder. And, finally, break though the clutter with simple and strategic communications. Use the above points as a thought stimulator, but don't go overboard. Just do it.

What follows is a 20-step **"PERSUASION GUIDE"** to help define your PMA, construct a response and implement the communication element of RadarScan.

Radar Scan Issues Management — *PERSUASION GUIDE*

1. Issue _____
   _____

2. What are the (audience's) existing...
   Belief(s) _____
   Attitude(s) _____
   Behavior _____
   Core values _____

3. What do we want them to be?
   Belief(s) _____
   Attitude(s) _____
   Behavior _____
   Core values _____
   Objective(s), winning: _____

4. What appeals/incentives would produce the desired result?
   _____

5. What is the audience's level of issue relevance and likelihood of elaboration?
   ❏ High   ❏ Moderate   ❏ Low

6. What is the intensity of issue relevance?
   ❏ High   ❏ Moderate   ❏ Low

7. Is audience understanding and education level on the issue high enough for persuasion to occur quickly (direct approach) or slowly (building block)?
   ❏ Direct approach   ❏ Building block

8. Is there a group consensus on the issue? _____
    If yes, is it the desired one? _____
    If no, what is the key point a consensus could be built upon? _____
    _____

9. Is there a need to direct the audience to selected aspects of the message in building block fashion? _____
    Selected _____ Full range _____

10. What level of message comprehension should be sought?
    Simple _____ Detailed _____

11. What are the strongest arguments? _____
    _____

12. What are the weaker arguments? _____

13. What is the optimum number of message arguments...Primary Message Array (PMA)? _____

14. After analyzing the audience's elaboration likelihood, and other factors in this model, what is the optimum frequency to send messages? _____

15. Rate the degree of complexity in persuading stakeholder.
    ❏ Minimal   ❏ Moderate   ❏ Strong

16. After analyzing the degree of complexity, and other factors in this model, what is the optimum number of sources?_____

17. Is there an opportunity to weave into text and leverage the personality quotient?   ❏ Yes   ❏ No

18. Which persuasion route is most appropriate?
    Systemic (detailed) _____
    Heuristic (rule of thumb) _____
    Affective (emotional) _____

19. What are the appropriate media choices? _____

_____

20. PRIMARY MESSAGE ARRAY – Contextualize the message to stakeholder's PERSPECTIVE: _____

_____

_____

Getting The Resources To Do The Job

It's easy to develop strategies and communications plans, but it's something else to fund them adequately to win. It's critical to conduct a "Resource Analysis" early, during planning for the action phase. This approach helps control expectations and leads to reasonable action plans.

The analysis must transcend the financial side of the resource equation. Take a look at this list of items needed to carry out the program:
1) Money
2) Over what period?
3) Research and Information
4) Skills/Expertise
5) Materials
6) Personnel
7) Support and clout internal and external to the organization
8) Coordination

Keep Information Coming In

Once into the action phase, it's important to keep information coming into the RadarScan System. In addition to the information gathering system explained in Chapter 5, the latest up-to-the-minute intelligence on the issue and its campaign can be picked up from calls into the office and communications on the Internet. Just as important as keeping information coming in during the action phase is to zealously maintain your support through communication, communication, and more communication. Send out regular UPDATES to stakeholders and "market" your success, but be careful not to overdo it. Periodically report progress on specific issues, both accomplishments and shortfalls.

When an issue starts to wind down, it's easy to shut down the engine. But stake-holders need to be informed—they know less than you and your team swimming in the issue's vortex. Evaluating what happened is a critical part of the issues management process. Sure, everyone involved will be happy to have the intensity go away, and formal evaluation is the last thing on most people's minds. This is especially true when you've been successful. The mindset then is, "What's there to evaluate?" On the other side, if you've experienced a disappointing outcome the tendency is to say, "Evaluate? What does it matter now?"

Both of these views are misguided and dangerous. The evaluation process is critical to put a final frame around the issue for the future. What do we have on our hands now that the issue has passed through resolution? Is the issue completely dead? What are the consequences to our organization? Should we continue to be involved? In what way? These questions are critical because most issues don't completely disappear. The evaluation process also helps an organization make adjustments in its issues management program for the future.

This important step of reviewing the issues management program is the focus of Chapter 9.

CHAPTER 9

The Evaluation Imperative

If you don't know where you are and if you don't know where you've been, arriving where you want to be becomes an improbable accident of sheer, dumb luck.

Program evaluation is the process that reveals whether or not you've succeeded in reaching objectives—or more typically, the degree to which you have succeeded. It is extraordinarily rare that everything you set out to accomplish will have been perfectly achieved. Executing evaluation is necessarily a retrospective process. Planning for it, however, has to be an integral part of program development, taken into account as each of the previous steps is executed.

This chapter relates to the **"REVIEW"** circle in the RadarScan Issues Management Model.

In addition to the content and structure of evaluation programs, it is important to take into account evaluation costs. The two, indeed, are largely inseparable. More content and more rigorous structure typically translate into higher costs. It is important to determine how much evaluation is necessary in relation to what the budget and the issue warrants, along with the need for information in order to craft future positions and response.

The evaluation element of an issues management project has three components:
* Status review
* Ongoing testing
* Summary review

Status Review

The status review provides a baseline against which program success can be evaluated. Fundamentally, it involves establishing where you and others are with regard to the issue; who those others are; and where the issue stands within the larger social, political and economic context that spawned it. For example, is legislation, regulation or some sort of judicial resolution likely? If so, when? Much of this work will already have been completed if you have been careful and thorough in executing earlier steps in the RadarScan Issues Management process. In particular, required information will have emerged from your environmental scanning and issue analysis. That same information, coupled with goal definition achieved in strategy development, provides critical guidance in, first, knowing against what your progress is to be measured, and, second, developing mechanisms for measurement.

Ongoing Testing

The entire notion of evaluation has to do with assessing where you are against where you want to be. But it's important to keep in mind that you may want to be in different places at different times over the course of an issues management program. Achievements are incremental, and program implementation is also incremental, and expensive. Reasonable prudence suggests you don't want to come to the conclusion of a program only to discover your goals haven't been reached. Avoiding that unhappy consequence is the objective of ongoing testing designed to measure incremental success.

As part of evaluation program design, it is important to specify intermediate points in program implementation at which progress will be measured. In some cases, it may be best to take stock at certain time intervals. In others, it may be more revealing to assess progress following completion of specific program components or phases. And, of course, the two may be inextricably linked. In any case, it is imperative that broad goals constructed as part of your strategy be broken into smaller pieces, or sets of sub-goals.

The reason for setting up sub-goals is that they provide a basis for measuring project success at intermediate points of implementation, allowing for midcourse corrections if necessary. It makes little sense to continue moving on a preordained path if the exercise is foredoomed to failure.

Summary Review

A summary review or evaluation is completed at the conclusion of the issues management program, with the objective of taking a broad look at what was achieved, what goals may not have been reached, and developing corrective measures to be taken in development of future issues management programs and their evaluation components.

Measuring Success

The way goals are defined can make a critical difference in whether or not you can reasonably measure how well you are doing. A goal statement saying, "We would like to see our opponents on this issue come to agree with us," is really pretty useless. First, no matter what you do, not all opponents will concur, and, second, there is no way to really know whether they do or not.

Some examples of better ways of stating goals may help, though in all cases the basic objective is to develop a statement that is susceptible to some kind of measurement. For instance: Following three months of program implementation, 30 percent of (a specified set of) stakeholders will agree with our position on (some sub-goal). Or, following three months of program implementation, 10 percent of previously uncommitted stakeholders will approve of our position on (some specified sub-goal or issue component). Or, following 180 days of program implementation, 35 percent more of (a specified set of stakeholders) will demonstrate (some desirable and previously unobserved behavior). Or, at the conclusion of the program, (some event or set of events will have occurred).

In each of the foregoing examples, however, there remains a missing piece. How do you determine that the specified shifts have indeed occurred? So let's take it one more time from the top, developing statements that include the methods we will employ in assessing success. Here are three examples:

Following three months of program implementation, 30 percent of (a specified set of) stakeholders will agree with our position on (some sub-goal), as measured by an independently designed and executed telephone survey involving a random sample.

Following three months of program implementation, 10 percent of previously uncommitted stakeholders will approve of our position on (some specified sub-goal or issue component) as measured by a direct mail survey involving the population of uncommitted, and designed and executed by an independent research firm.

> — *Note that this one presents some additional problems that are resolvable only at some considerable cost; you have to know how many uncommitted you started with, and have a mail list for all of them.*

Following 180 days of program implementation, 35 percent more of (a specified set of stakeholders) will demonstrate (some desirable and previously unobserved behavior), as measured by observation (of that behavior).

— *Here, you have to know how many among the specified set of stakeholders demonstrated the behavior before you launched your program.*

Among the implications—both for evaluation and for construction of the issues management program of which it is a part—is that "before-and-after" testing may be required to determine how much progress has been made. Further, in order to be sure observed changes are attributable to your program, it may be necessary to establish experimental and control groups, the first of which is exposed to the message, and the latter not.

It's clear that the process can become about as intricate as you may want to make it, and deciding how you are going to proceed is linked to how much money you have, how much of it you want to spend on evaluation, how much information is enough and how good is good enough. Of course, accountability to a board of directors, person, or body will also dictate the evaluation required. The accompanying politics, to the extent they exist, must also be dealt with to maintain support of your issues management efforts.

Evaluation Tools

Similarly, evaluation tools are tied to the amount, sort and quality of information you require, as well as to what may be suggested by program objectives. Evaluation research, like most other kinds, can be **Exploratory** (determining what of interest is at work in the environment), **Descriptive** (describing what appears to be happening) and **Explanatory** (offering explanations for what is occurring).

It may well be the case that different goals suggest different evaluation tactics and strategies. In any event, one or more of the following research approaches may be relevant. The list is divided according to type of research, with some specific methods indicated for each.

Quantitative Research

Quantitative research by definition involves counting, though the sort of counting required can be pretty daunting. Data analysis and reporting typically involve statistical treatments. Types of research methods lending themselves to quantitative methods include:

- Telephone surveys
- Direct mail surveys
- "House-to-House" surveys
- Person-in-the-street surveys
- Content analysis (of messages, mediated or otherwise)

Among the weakness of this kind of research (excepting content analysis) is that respondents are required to conform their answers to questions and scales (How do you feel on a scale of 1-5 about the issue?) that may have little or no relevance to their own perception of reality.

Qualitative Research

The distinction between qualitative and quantitative research is both fundamental and fairly obvious. With qualitative research, the preoccupation is with content of a phenomenon—how or what one feels or believes about an issue. In many cases, however, qualitative research methods do not necessarily depart dramatically from those involved in quantitative evaluations. Surveys may also be a crucial ingredient in qualitative work. The difference is largely in how the survey instrument is constructed, how the questions are phrased. Qualitatively oriented questionnaires are characterized by inquiries asking how respondents feel or believe about certain events, ways in which they have been handled and, perhaps, ways in which they should be handled. Questions are open-ended, so response options are not constrained, and answers may be open to considerable interpretation.

Another differentiation between quantitative and qualitative research is in the scope and consequent projectability. Qualitative research typically involves a smaller sample and is NOT projectable in a statistical sense. Content analysis can be applied here as well, with the analysis focusing on qualitative characteristics of the response, rather than, for example, how many times certain words appear in a newspaper article or other text. Additionally, qualitative analysis may involve Delphi Panels and participant observation.

In the use of **Delphi Panels,** experts, frequently senior executives and academics, are asked to evaluate the status of an event, program or project, and provide direction with regard to things that either should or shouldn't be done. As the title implies, this sort of research is oracular—predictive—and may be especially useful in interrogating the environment, with the objective of applying answers to issues management program construction. Delphi research employs recursive methodology—sending out an information frame or questionnaire to a select group whose input is sought, interpreting responses, developing a second instrument that permits group members to react and refine their responses in light of their colleagues' responses, and so on, until an acceptable level of clarity or consensus is reached.

Participant observation requires trained researchers to become involved in activities related to the issue, observing the relevant behaviors of stakeholders, with the objective of gaining keener insights into motivations and suggesting appropriate responses. By way of example, participant observation might be useful in evaluating a program directed at educating consumers on ways of selecting quality products. The question posed, and presumably answerable employing this method, has to do with whether observed consumers employ the guidance in making purchase decisions.

It bears remembering that, in many cases, available methods can be linked—and ideally often should be—in highly complementary ways. How much linkage is possible relates to available dollars and the quality/quantity of information required to guide the organization in its issues management work.

Evaluating The Team

Evaluating and compensating the issues management team is a difficult, but important task. Providing incentive is key to maximizing results from those working on the issues. The best approach is to develop a long-range perspective toward compensation so results can be measured and rewarded over time.

Evaluation of the team also allows the organization to establish an "accountability culture" to minimize "wheel turning" issues management activities that don't deliver value and results commensurate to the investment.

Frequently, a positive evaluation is dependent upon "it"—whatever you wanted to avoid—being successfully avoided. Other times, evaluation relies upon a "bottom line" measurement, asking if the result is harmony between the organization and its stakeholders, or if the organization and issue team did what they set out to do. And whether or not that led to harmony.

Measurement should be tied to overall objectives, with specific rewards to issues management team members.

The evaluation step discussed in this chapter is critical to an organization's success at managing issues in two areas: 1) contextualizing the issue at the end stages in order to develop further involvement (if any), and 2) learning from the experience for future issues management efforts as the process starts up again and new issues appear on the radar screen. One thing is certain. New issues will always appear, and the need to keep the issues management program top of mind and well oiled—and getting better after each effort— is an imperative for success.

To help you do that, the final chapter summarizes the RadarScan Issues Management Model.

CHAPTER 10

Summary

Take action and go!

The discipline of managing issues successfully is complex and difficult. To be good at it, an organization must commit to a program and work it diligently through all of the steps even when the information is short and the process imperfect. RadarScan Issues Management can be summarized by that commitment and a bias toward taking action, no matter what.

As I said in the preface, after managing dozens of issues over 10 years I've learned how important it is to get involved early and **act**, even when it doesn't feel right…to anticipate issues, paint scenarios and project trajectories. Unfortunately, many of us can't get to the macro level and instead focus on the day-to-day nuts and bolts of running the business. Hopefully, by now you've seen the need to be out front early on issues and learned how to develop this ANTICIPATORY ORIENTATION.

But that's just the first step in a two-step process. The critical second step is "putting something in play" and TAKING ACTION! Even when it doesn't look like you have enough information, make a move and get started.

Go! Begin To Begin!

Once the goals and strategies are established, it's time to start the action machine. Regardless of the strategies and tactics you choose, you need to seize the initiative and go…and go early.

The initial thrust and consequent commitment it triggers always feel awkward. We fill our minds with negative self talk like, "What if the stakeholder does this, or the strategy fails, or they move and destroy our chances before we even start?" I've never worked on an issue where I didn't feel queasy in the beginning. But I haven't lost one yet by going out early and hard.

We all want to wait until everyone and everything lines up in perfect order and alignment so we can go. Forget it! It will never happen. Force the beginning and break the seal. Begin to begin. Begin the exploration and start "moving the dirt."

The "move the dirt" metaphor and its application to issues management came to me one day while I watched a man prepare to hop on a huge earth mover and tackle a piece of land with hills, ruts, trees, concrete and many other obstacles.

Before he started, I asked him how he knew where to start and what to do with so many unknowns in his path. He said the plans submitted by the engineers provided a general path for him to follow, but it wasn't until he started moving the dirt that he really knew what to do.

He kept repeating that line, "You've got to move the dirt. You've got to move the dirt." He told me each time he moved some dirt he learned a little more about the property. How it sloped. What was underneath each section. Where the danger spots were lurking. And how to maximize his efforts in the most efficient manner possible.

Surprised at his response, I asked him when he would have enough experience to feel more confident before he started the project. He replied assertively, "I've been doing this for 32 years and I'm an expert. If I waited for the day I knew everything about the property and how to shape it, I would never get on the tractor."

That story says it all. The only way to get there is to begin moving dirt, no matter how uncertain and menacing the terrain looks. It's action past risk and beyond fear. It's a series of iterative steps, each building on the other. It's exploration before all of the answers are in. It's go, and go quick out of the starting blocks.

Sounds too easy? How do you pull it off? Here are my **Top 10 Strategies** for getting RadarScan Issues Management "in play," (most issues will use several in a variety of combinations):

1. Strategic Positioning
   Even though it's important to go out early, often without an ideal information base, you still need a strategic position to guide the effort. Develop it carefully, assiduously and purposefully. To do otherwise is a recipe for disaster.

2. Develop An Identity
   Develop an issue campaign identity with a logo. Make it arresting, impactful and representative of your position on the issue. Plaster it everywhere. Don't let any communication into the system without the logo.

3. Be First...Seize The Initiative
   Move first. Seize the initiative by acting ahead of the events to neutralize the effectiveness of the other side or to preclude their taking any action at all.

4. <u>Frame It Your Way</u>
   Break the pattern. Do something different. Make a statement on a totally new track. Have a new person from another angle make a statement. Instead of fighting over the same points on the same field, shift the focus to another field. Move away from head-on confrontation to a different spot in the road. Most issues are driven by emotion and veer away from facts to ambiguities and unfocused discourse.

   Organizations that "frame it their way" force the other side to be specific and move them off the emotional and unfocused track. The first step in this process is to isolate the specific issue and its parameters instead of focusing on the opposition and its ideology, ethnicity, structure or practices. Identify exactly what the other side wants. Even though the opposition's demands are probably part of a bigger agenda, it's critical to keep the focus on the issue in order to avoid making mistakes in attacking the wrong things. The immediate job is to quickly get a handle on the issue at stake and what is wanted in particular. Counter facts with facts. Then mount your response and offensive strategies to counter, in the strongest and most strategic way, the specifics surrounding the issue.

5. <u>Draw New Boundaries</u>
   Redraw the playing field boundaries to extend time, reorient the focus, take the opponent to another spot. Delay. Detour. Start a back fire. Go off on a tangent from the main issue. Interrupt the other side's pattern and strategic train of thought. Draw the opposition's resources and attention away from the initial focus. Identify and disarm the fulcrum point or person on the issue.

6. <u>Maneuver & Surprise</u>
   Surprise is often a great start to an issues management campaign. Make them respond to you! A wild angle, way off the conventional track or different from what the other side would expect, can shift the issue's equilibrium and position it more to your advantage. The Maneuver & Surprise strategy secures quick initial control of the issue as you come out of the blocks fast and aggressively with heavy artillery that envelopes the other side. It's possible to completely overwhelm the opponent with an aggressive communications campaign that pens them in and ties them up. One of the benefits of this approach is that the other side won't know how many bullets are in

your gun and will assume that "it must be plenty full if they came out like this." Maneuver & Surprise as a strategy is an extremely difficult and risky gambit that demands an intensive commitment of resources, and a little luck to pull off.

7. Roll Over

There are times when the best approach is to passively roll over and do absolutely nothing. This is a passive strategy by design, but not apathy, stonewalling or conceding a loss. If you've decided strategically to let the other side set the table, this approach gives you a chance to step back and see how the issue unfolds and to force the other side's hand. In the Roll Over mode, you decide what to respond to, when to do it, and how to do it. By waiting to see how the issue unfolds, you can maximize your impact by choosing the areas where you can score points.

Roll Over is a risky approach, but effective if your position is solid. Often the challenge to this approach comes from within, especially on emotional issues, when the CEO or board wants to slam the other side and "set the record straight."

8. Stalk, Then Pounce

Just like a cat who sizes up its prey and then pounces for the kill, sometimes it's a good idea to hold back some parts of your strategy and then pounce later. This approach keeps you from revealing your entire strategy at one time and you can wait for a "special opportunity" after you see the flaws in the other side. Let the other side go crazy and blow up so they will expose their strategy and its weaknesses in the process. Then you can say, "Thanks for bringing this important issue out into the open so we can respond. Here's our story..." Obviously, this approach only applies when you don't have to "set the table" and control the issue and its debate.

9. Join Forces!

Build a bigger force than you could on your own by joining forces with other stakeholders on the issue. An Issues Alliance Coalition is a divergent team representing the various sides of the issue; yes, maybe even the enemy! Open up, let them in, they'll strengthen the process and help. Close them out and you could be hurt.

The credibility of Issue Alliance participants is critical during the discussion process and into the implementation and resolution stages. Control must be shared with equal access information and dialog with all the lights on, even though this is anathema to many organizations which constantly seek a shield to keep everyone and everything out.

The coalition participants bundle together credible players representing various interests seeking common ground and a mutually beneficial, win-win solution. The purpose must be to impact the issue's outcome and arrive at the desired end state. There should be no doubt what the specific goals are and what specific behaviors the group is trying to induce. The group must have a strategic purpose and each member must have a genuine stake in the issue. Get agreement on goals and strategies up front and then manage expectations. Be realistic about what can be achieved. Define success and winning so you can recognize success.

Where do coalition members come from? They are opinion leaders on an issue who are "tired of the fight." Candidates come from organizations where they can't be a force alone, or they represent different views, perspectives and disciplines that broaden and strengthen the effort to increase the odds of prevailing. Remember that each member brings to the table his or her own agenda and baggage, but beware of dangerous bedfellows that will tarnish you through "guilt by association."

10. Scorched Earth

    Press, Press, Press. Never stop the water flowing. This transcends the message, the media, and frequency of communication. The Scorched Earth strategy is perfect for issues in which you've got nothing to lose by exploding. Scorch works very well when the only way to win is to radically alter the focus and context of the issue.

Remember the RadarScan Issues Management TENETS:

1. There is no such thing as on time; there is only early and late.

2. Traditional, linear structure doesn't work well in an amorphous, virtual environment. Get rid of the yellow chairs. Challenge assumptions and use virtual teams in managing issues.

3. It may be true, as the hippie said, that everybody has to be somewhere, but soul's the secret to getting where you want to be.

4. There are better options than probable death and certain death. Identify strategic impact issues, and deal with them.

5. People may be created equal, but information is NOT. Scan the environment for information that is critical to YOUR success.

6. Everything is composed of relationships, and they are always more convoluted than you thought they were.

7. It's a lot more like skeet shooting than firing at still targets; everything has a distressing tendency to keep moving.

8. You've succeeded if, at the end, they believe they won.

9. Evaluate. If you don't know where you are and if you don't know where you've been, arriving where you want to be becomes an improbable accident of sheer, dumb luck.

10. Take action and go!

Welcome to the Change Age and good luck with your issues management program.

APPENDIX A

RadarScan
Issues Management Model

Circle 1

SOUL

Vision & Values

- What do we stand for?
- What's important?
- Where are we going?
- When do we want to arrive there?

"IT'S NOT WHERE THE PUCK IS .....IT'S WHERE IT WILL BE."

CHALLENGE ASSUMPTIONS

Decision Point: Decide what you stand for since **SOUL** directs what occurs in each area of Issues Management.

Circle 2

SCAN

SEARCHING FOR THE
STRATEGIC IMPACT ISSUES

What will sink the ship?

- Specify incoming data conduits
- Identify monitors for conduits
- Develop database
- Prioritize issues

Decision Point: Continue to
Scan/Monitor and proceed to
Analysis

Circle 3

ANALYZE

Interpretative Tools
- Scenario Forecast
- Trend Analysis
- Focus Groups
- Trajectory
- Force Field

Assess Issue
- Probability
- Impact
- Risk

Issue Life Cycle
- Emerging
- Forming
- Building
- Exploding
- Drifting
- Resolving

Target Profile
- Demographic
- Psychographic
- Lifestyle
- Attitude Continuum
- Perception Chasm
- Position on Issue

ISSUE SUMMARY

Decision Point: Continue to
Scan/Monitor or proceed to
ACTION

Circle 4

STRATEGY

DEFINE GOALS

Response Options

- Strategic positioning
- Develop campaign identity
- Be first, seize initiative
- Frame it your way
- Draw your own boundaries
- Maneuver & surprise
- Roll over
- Stalk & Pounce
- Join forces
- Scorched earth

Resources Availability

- Human
- Financial

Options/Implications

Decision Point: Select options or stop

Circle 5

ACTION

CONSTRUCT RESPONSE

Factors
- Persuasion pathway
- Method of dissemination
- Method of reception
- Recipient retention
- Recipient beliefs
- Recipient attitudes
- Recipient behaviors
- Message timing

Stakeholder Stratification
- Support
- Oppose
- Neutral

Primary Message Array
- Simple messages
- Break the clutter

Decision Point: Put action in play or stop

Circle 6

REVIEW

Revisit Goals

Develop Related Measures

Assess Success Through
- Mid course corrections
- Program conclusion

Evaluation Methods
(quantitative & qualitative)
- Surveys
- Delphi panels

Decision Point: Select/implement
evaluation protocols

Circle 1

SOUL
Vision & Values
- What do we stand for?
- What's important?
- Where are we going?
- When do we want to arrive there?

"IT'S NOT WHERE THE PUCK IS .....IT'S WHERE IT WILL BE."

CHALLENGE ASSUMPTIONS

Decision Point: Decide what you stand for since **SOUL** directs what occurs in each area of Issues Management.

Circle 2

SCAN
SEARCHING FOR THE STRATEGIC IMPACT ISSUES

What will sink the ship?
- Specify incoming data conduits
- Identify monitors for conduits
- Develop database
- Prioritize issues

Decision Point: Continue to Scan/Monitor and proceed to Analysis

Circle 3

ANALYZE

Interpretative Tools
- Scenario Forecast
- Trend Analysis
- Focus Groups
- Trajectory
- Force Field

Target Profile
- Demographic
- Psychographic
- Lifestyle
- Attitude Continuum
- Perception Chasm
- Position on Issue

Assess Issue
- Probability
- Impact
- Risk

Issue Life Cycle
- Emerging
- Forming
- Building
- Exploding
- Drifting
- Resolving

ISSUE SUMMARY

Decision Point: Continue to Scan/Monitor or proceed to **ACTION**

Circle 4

STRATEGY

Response Options
- Strategic positioning
- Develop campaign identity
- Be first, seize initiative
- Frame it your way
- Draw your own boundaries
- Maneuver & surprise
- Roll over
- Stalk & Pounce
- Join forces
- Scorched earth

Resources Availability
- Human
- Financial

Options/ Implications

DEFINE GOALS

Decision Point: Select options or stop

Circle 5

ACTION

Factors
- Persuasion pathway
- Method of dissemination
- Method of reception
- Recipient retention
- Recipient beliefs
- Recipient attitudes
- Recipient behaviors
- Message timing

Stakeholder Stratification
- Support
- Oppose
- Neutral

Primary Message Array
- Simple messages
- Break the clutter

CONSTRUCT RESPONSE

Decision Point: Put action in play or stop

Circle 6

REVIEW
Revisit Goals
Develop Related Measures
Assess Success Through
- Mid course corrections
- Program conclusion

Evaluation Methods
(quantitative & qualitative)
- Surveys
- Delphi panels

Decision Point: Select/implement evaluation protocols

INDEX